Living in Parentheses

Living in Parentheses

*Cancer
And Who
You Are*

Rose Rappaport

Full Court Press
Englewood Cliffs, New Jersey

First Edition

Copyright © 2012 by Harvey Rappaport

All rights reserved. No part of this book may be reproduced or transmitted in any form or by any means electronic or mechanical, including by photocopying, by recording, or by any information storage and retrieval system, without the express permission of the author and publisher, except where permitted by law.

Published in the United States of America
by Full Court Press, 601 Palisade Avenue
Englewood Cliffs, NJ 07632
www.fcpressnj.com

ISBN 978-0-9849536-3-9
Library of Congress Catalog No. 2012934588

*Cover Photograph, "Door Brace, Margaretville, NY,"
Copyright © 2006 Barry Sheinkopf*

Author Photograph by Harvery Rappaport

*Editing and Book Design by Barry Sheinkopf for Bookshapers
www.bookshapers.com*

Colophon by Liz Sedlack

Foreword

As the challenges of the cancer kept coming, Rose always remained very positive. She was determined not to let it rob her of things she loved to do. There were many things that struck me as the last few months flew by. Two of them were some of the hardest to deal with. The pain and the drugs taken to alleviate it kept Rose from reading and writing. Seeing her lose concentration and focus to do these things just broke my heart even more.

For Rose, reading was as much part of life as breathing. You couldn't ask her to stop breathing just as you could not ask to stop reading. I would often times tease her about how ingrained reading was to her. It was almost an addiction. Even if we were just out to the cleaners and bank, a book was in her hand so that any spare moment could be utilized to get through another page. In better times when we went to bed, I cannot remember a single night when the lamp by her bedside didn't stay on for some significant period so she could get to the end of a chapter. Her reading covered everything from novels to self help to religion. Just about any subject was cause to pick up another book. For her, there was nothing better than wandering the tables and aisles at Barnes & Noble. It was like watching a kid in a candy store.

Writing came to her just within the past couple of years. In an odd way, I believe hearing the voices of so many writers prompted her to think about her own voice. Once she was diagnosed, the call to get her thoughts out became louder. She began by attending the Writing Center run by Barry Sheinkopf. Tentatively and somewhat timidly, she started to write. It was interesting to hear her talk about it. On the one hand, she felt the writing was solely for her but as her stories were read in class, she secretly took great pleasure in knowing others were moved by what she had to say. She related to me there was talk in class of putting her essays together in a book. When she said this, it was in a slightly softer voice as somehow saying it out loud might mean failure if it never came to pass.

And that brings us to where we are now. With Barry's help, we're bringing Rose's voice to the world again. As I said in announcing her death, Rose was a teacher in all aspects of the word. I hope you will learn from her again as you read these essays.

Rose and I always said one of the reasons we were blessed was because of the many angels we met during this journey. We were referring to the countless people who helped and supported us along the way. It would be impossible to thank them all here. However, I would like to cite her three primary physicians at Sloan Kettering for their tireless effort on her behalf. They are Eileen O'Reilly, Kenneth Cubert, and William Breitbart. To them and the rest of the angels, God bless you all.

—Harvey Rappaport

Editor's Note

The order of these observations, and their arrangement into categories, are mine. I urged Rose to choose them in the months before her death, and she found the challenge intriguing, but she never got around to it. Since any such scheme exists in the first place, however, solely to illuminate the thought it frames—and since I can claim without reservation that Rose's work casts pretty vast illumination on its own—I'm confident that my efforts have not dimmed its diamond glow.

—Barry Sheinkopf

Contents

AWARENESS

Kaleidoscope, *3*
Uncharted, *6*
The "C" Word, *8*
Normal, *11*
Living in Parentheses, *14*
The Ultimate Reality Show, *16*
Things Happen, *17*
Silence, *18*

BODY IMAGE

Hair Today, Gone Tomorrow, *23*
Naked Eyes, *30*

TREATMENT

The Procedure, *35*
Don't Know What to Say, *40*
The Wave, *42*
Scans, *45*
Resilience, *47*
June 2, 2007, *50*
Until, *53*

FAMILY

Who Will Prevail?, *59*
A Tale of Two Brothers, *61*
Comments, *66*
John, *70*

MOOD

Work, *75*
Bubbles, *78*
A Gift, *81*
That Which Cannot Be Named, *84*
Just What Is Hope?, *87*

PAIN

Jellyfish, *91*
Ice Water, *92*

LOVE

A Dream Come True, *99*
Intimacy, *101*
Anniversary, *104*
Soulmates, *107*

CONNECTIONS

My Friend Albert, *111*
An Encounter, *116*
We, *119*
The Strings of Friendship, *123*

SLEEP

Will I Know?, *129*
Insomnia, *131*

LIFE AND DEATH

Just a Movie, *135*
We'll See, *136*
Who Am I?, *138*
Surrender, *141*
Last Notes, *144*

Awareness

Kaleidoscope

Lately my life seems like a movie—though not evil, I'm the witch in *The Wizard of Oz*, melting. The me I knew is being told I no longer exist. The rage is beyond comprehension. From angry tears to total withdrawal, I no longer know who I am.

Yet in my more rational moments, I realize that life is seldom tidy, that, like a kaleidoscope of interlinked pieces, my life refuses to remain in focus. The pieces are still there, they interact with one another, and, in that interaction, reality changes. Give the kaleidoscope one small twist, and in an instant the pieces have shifted into another pattern, one I do not recognize or particularly favor.

This condition—for what else can it be?—is the result of being unemployed in my fifties. When I was young, I had "potential". Opportunities were available and my talents sought. Job criteria included, then as now, one or two job skills as yet unacquired. No problem, my potential, my ability to think, to learn and figure them out, was an acceptable barometer. If I could do what I had already done, my potential would bring me through.

My career progressed. Potential morphed into experience—not just in business, but in life. People wanted me to mentor them. I had arrived.

With the loss of my corporate position at the half-century mark, it appears potential evaporates no matter what your track record, no matter the vibrancy of your spirit or passion for making a difference. At least that's the message society transmits. Suddenly you no longer fit the bill.

Recently I read an article actually naming this now-frequent occurrence "the fertile void."

It struck me that, if there was a name for "it," I was not alone. Amazingly I began to see my circumstance in a totally different light. Instead of ranting about the unfairness and blaming society, I saw that I had been given a unique opportunity to change a few things. The lens of the kaleidoscope had shifted and I had been given a Do Over—a chance to do some of the things on my mental wish list. What I had once viewed as a cursed event was now a blessing.

I began quickly—nothing extreme, mostly external changes. Time at the gym to get the bod in better shape topped the list. All those layers in my hair could now be grown out without fear of looking unkempt.

A change in wardrobe allowed me to give lots of clothes to those in need and gave me a chance to experiment with some new styles and colors.

Pleased with the outward transformation, I moved into the inner depths. This took more courage.

The brain, I learned, is like any muscle: If you don't use it, it too can get flabby. I decided to take the pent-up potential and apply my talents to teaching at university level. I learned my experience had a value that was not written into the textbooks.

I discovered the young may have a longer runway, but do not necessarily have the equipment to arrive at the desired destination fully intact. I could help guide them by providing reality testing for the theories. A wonderful byproduct was the easy camaraderie that developed with my students. My energy soared; my outlook and conversations brighten. There was more to consider than I'd originally thought.

Pressing further, I reviewed my "potential" in the light of what I loved to do best, which prompted me to obtain a certification in career coaching. A few more workshops at the small business association, and I launched Human Capital Partnership, a management consulting and coaching practice. I was an entrepreneur.

My efforts to push my potential have lead me to take a writing course, the result of which is this article.

Usually what follows is a list of "Dos" that instruct the reader on how to follow "my proven model of success." You will not find instructions here. The only thing that needs to happen is a change of mindset—that's really all it takes, and only you can decide when you are ready.

Just one turn of the kaleidoscope lens and your perspective can change. So the next time life gives you an unexpected twist, have the courage to look beyond to the possibilities of a new life pattern, perhaps one you never thought could be yours.

Uncharted

Lately when I cannot sleep, I find myself crafting outlines of essays I should write: a new insight, an experience that has a different meaning now, a chance meeting with a friend who is surprised I am still around and looking 'normal.'

In *The Courage to Create*, Rollo May wrote, "We cannot will [ourselves] to have insights. We cannot will creativity. But we can will to give ourselves to the encounter with intensity of dedication and commitment."

Commitment to the encounter or the experience must include deep, honest recognition of embedded emotions and undeveloped ideas and, yes, absurd possibilities, and, then again, a good dose of risk taking.

I have re-read some of my essays and find I am surprised by the touch they have on my heart. Certainly I would never consider myself a writer. If anything, I have always thought of myself as more verbal—possessing the fairly uncommon gift of speaking my mind without offending. I always considered this a skill honed through the countless coaching sessions in my professional human resource role.

The ability to listen intently and reflect back without imposing your choice of options, the ability to dissect another's circumstance and outline the various options available and their possible outcome or impact, has been one of my strong skills. But this opportunity, and the commitment to delve deep into my innermost thinking, to share the reality of this disease and me, are uncharted waters.

At times I feel like a pioneer entering the murky realm of the inner self and reporting back to those on the surface awarenesses and discoveries opaque to healthy people. As I struggle, I manage to send back a note tied to a carrier pigeon. I am uncertain where the pigeon will land or whether you will understand attempts to describe this deeper knowledge. Scrooge, in *A Christmas Carol*, also saw things and lived through events hidden from the routine, the hectic storm, of life. At times I am desperate to educate those willing to pause and listen. The inner self possesses the answers to a myriad of life issues. Take the time, it calls out, to enter, to knock on the door of self-knowledge, to know who you really are.

It's amazing what you can discover.

The "C" Word

THE ONCE DREADED "C" word is no longer a death sentence according to National Cancer Institute. News about cancer, it seems, is everywhere. Last month Elizabeth Edwards' breast cancer recurred, and then Tony Snow, the president's press secretary, said his colon cancer had returned. Last Wednesday Fred Thompson, a possible presidential candidate, said he has had lymphoma.

The newsmagazine shows talk about all of these diseases, and about medical science making major strides in treatment and palliative care. It seems once a celebrity or politician is diagnosed, research dollars become available. By comparison, in the twenty-plus months since my own diagnosis, I have not seen one news report, and have read few articles, on pancreatic cancer—I suppose the fact that ninety-six percent of patients don't even survive one year has something to do with it. New drug treatments are the application of off-label protocols to the standard regimen for this type of cancer.

Whenever I participate in fund-raising walks, most of the walkers are doing so in memory of a loved one. Few survivors have the strength to venture forth and join the walk.

To a certain extent, it's a crap shoot (or "a matter of will," in effect the same thing). The power of human resilience, as well as the depth of our fragility, is so unpredictable, you can never tell how a person pushed to extremes will behave

Pancreatic cancer is what it is. I decided long ago that statistics were averages, and that I have a choice about how I choose to deal with my circumstance. In this age of spin and individual truths, authenticity is the real deal, speaking up for what you believe in refusing to be ruled by the status quo or the commonplace. For me, authenticity is also provocative; it slices through the bull, jolts the unexpecting, is a moment of audacious originality. It is the alignment of thought and action with your vision and your values—the ability to be who you are in the world when it matters most.

Phil Jackson, coach of the Los Angeles Lakers, is quoted as saying. "You have to trust your inner knowing. If you have a clear mind, you won't have to search for direction. Direction will come to you."

So what is this inner knowing? Is it the brain? The mind? What is a "mind"? Does it exist separate from the heart? Is that just an organ to pump blood?

When I cling to myself, I feel neurotic, alienated, and insecure. When I let myself go, I begin to realize how fully a part of a grander scheme I am and will always remain. I remember reading somewhere in the work of a contemporary French mystic: *Il y a en moi quelque chose plus mot que moi-meme*: "There is in me something more me than myself." I am grateful for this energy but also confused and frustrated by it. Living consciously involves being genuine, listening and responding to others honestly and openly, being in the moment. It's about courage.

When we are at the top of our game, we radiate large amounts of energy. When this energy is directed toward some important task, good things happen. We experience success, learn and grow, gain new perspective. Can this energy be applied to my situation? Is this energy what they call *consciousness*?

I've been reading about this mysterious element. Often the books are beyond my understanding. So far, I have been able to discern that consciousness is very organic, an immeasurable element of which consists of ourselves. It is a force so powerful that I am incapable of comprehending its depth through the puny instrument of my solitary mind.

Some humans purport to understand it in a more precise way. I just give it respect and think of it as living in me as well as everywhere else. When I focus beyond me, my ego, my self, then suddenly I have access to a much grander form of awareness. It includes what I see and feel and what I cannot see but believe exists. It will far outlast my physical being. I am part of everything and yet uniquely me. It is the core of a person.

For me this authentic self begins with acting as if something were the case, to fake it till you make it so. I believe we are what we do with our intention, and it is my intention to live a healthy, happy, fulfilled life.

Normal

As I type the title of this piece, I shake my head and wonder if I will ever truly know "normal" again. Having had a life-threatening illness for the past two years has redefined the word—though maybe I do know what normal is, only it's changed so much it's hard to recognize!

I have already written about how each cancer, each treatment protocol, and each patient's reactions are unique. Part of my decision to keep to a regular schedule of activities has worked for Harvey and me. When you have cancer you become totally immersed. You are either getting ready for treatment, in it, or coming off it. I now have two and half shelves in my walk-in closet that would make a pharmacist proud. Some drugs are in current use, others abandoned because of adverse reactions. I was either too nauseated, too hyper, or drugged out. When questioned about what I am currently taking, Harvey recalls what I've taken, why it was prescribed, and the results. Each multisyllabic drug label also contains a lay person's term for it, and what is used for. The slightest change in protocol can draw today's "new normal" into chaos.

Some of our activities are patterned, like going to the gym each morning. I can't perform as I used to, but I do what I can. That usually consists of half an hour on the treadmill or elliptical machine, and a forty-five minutes weight workout on a specific body part. I want to keep my body strong to counteract the effects of the toxic substances that routinely flood it.

Part of the old "normal" was my love of learning and trying new things. To this end, I have enrolled in two workshops. The first is an on-line conference call on the subject of Abundance Intelligence. Like-minded individuals meet on a bridge line and discuss the illusions of scarcity thinking and the attributes of abundance. I have a randomly assigned partner to work through the fieldwork questions and exercises. The one I have now is my second; the first found my enthusiasm for the work an intrusion into *his* work-and-life schedule. I love the dialogue, and although I only know the participants electronically, several have reached out to make a more personal contact. You cannot be authentic and hide the facts of a serious medical circumstance. Your perspective is altered.

The second workshop is live and meets once a week on Tuesday mornings. I attend The Writing Center—an experience like no other. The studio is in the basement of a local real estate company. The walls are covered with notices and published articles by class attendees. Some are yellowing and curl at the edges. The bookshelves are packed with reference and writer/agent guides and directories. There is an assortment of photographs taken by the founder and guru Barry Sheinkopf.

I love this class for two main reasons, Barry and the attendees. Barry is a ruggedly handsome man with a flair for drama and storytelling. Before class, he picks his guitar and sings the emotion-filled words of Kris Kristofferson. As the class slowly comes together, conversations move to the subject of writing. Barry reads each work in the voice of the character, turning three-dimensional characters into textured living beings. He provides richness beyond grammar and punctuation corrections for each student. Quite often authors are recommended who illustrate the teaching point. Barry also relates the history and provides the back story to the noted work. Comments on culture, history, current events, are a natural part of each class. Quotes in Latin, detailed references from the Romance languages, are sprinkled throughout. Barry's teaching style is organic and energizing, filled with a congeries of facts and stories that lead each student to enter a doorway of learning and self-discovery.

The second reason I enjoy this class is my fellow attendees. Each is interesting, not just for his or her writing abilities, but for the glimpses of personal history and current life. Most have known each other for years. If someone in the group mentions the punch line, they all know the joke. They have welcomed me into their group and provided much needed encouragement, not just for my writing, but in the form of compassionate words about my illness.

I have missed the camaraderie that exists in being at work. This group is a partial replacement in providing my brain with stimulation and new learning and, more importantly, reviving my spirit.

If this is the new "normal", I welcome it with open arms.

Living in Parentheses

A *PARENTHESIS*, IN FORMAL grammar, is "that part of a sentence which is enclosed, inserted in, or attached to an already completed thought."

For me, a diagnosis of pancreatic cancer has metaphorically been inserted into an already full life. It has changed the texture but not the substance of my daily living. The decision to write about the diagnostic impact on ordinarily taken-for-granted events may be thought provoking.

Trying to write for the first time can be daunting. People with experience tell novices to "write about what they know." My previous attempts to turn out business articles with a fresh perspective resulted in a feeling that I was "reporting"—the writing was flat, my voice stilted. I have come to realize that the "juice" in writing comes from what you don't know—from encountering the new, the mystery of discovery, which will draw the reader into new understanding. But it is not just the reader who comes to new understanding. My decision to write about the most recent twenty-five months of my life—to think I might have something meaningful to say—has in itself been a discovery. It has required a pause in the drama of the current circumstance, a pulling back to consider what exactly is going on. The "pause" was, to an extent, forced on me.

On June 2, 2005, I was diagnosed with fourth stage pancreatic cancer. Cancer is the biggest challenge I have faced—not losing forty pounds, not losing my corporate job, starting a new business, or reinventing myself. This is personal, and it is painful. Yet the truly great and valuable lessons we learn in life are often learned through pain. Once you hear that word—cancer—your entire life splits into life before and life after the diagnosis. The world, however, does not change because you have cancer. The only world that changes is yours, for illness is the great equalizer. It doesn't matter who you are rich or poor, young or old, fat or thin—sick is sick.

The Ultimate Reality Show

EACH GENERATION HAS ITS own form of entertainment—those exhibitions that titillate the senses, that allow the mind to lose its sense of the mundane and heighten either the excitement or pleasure zones. Movies are promoted as *more realistic*; the technical displays on the screen cause one to cover the eyes. Not to be outdone, television has produced the *Reality Show*.

At first these were glimpses into the world of a celebrity. The more bizarre, the more intrigued the viewer. In antiquity, the Romans had the Coliseum, with the goring of Christians and gladiator battles. The more the voyeur can feel, the better the ratings. Yet it strikes me that most of us live our lives in a state of semi-unconsciousness. We navigate through life performing those behaviors that our family or society expect from us. Rarely do we stop to consider the *why* behind the action. We are caught in our own reality show.

Things Happen

THINGS HAPPEN—AS A blessing or as a burden. The question is not, *Why did it happen? Why this way? Why me?* or *What is the price I must pay?* It is simply, *How am I making use of it?*, and about that there is only one who can judge.

I told myself I would accept the decision of fate. But keeping that promise becomes increasingly shaky when I realize how attached I am to the old life, which has made me who I am. The me I must leave behind in so many ways...it's shocking!

It feels like an amputation to part with the fathomed feelings of a life that once was—yet to move forward, the entirety of the former must be given up, and so the tears.

Silence

I've been on this treatment protocol for eleven months. That's chemo every other week. Usually side effects happen immediately.

Not to me.

My oncologist told me I've taken each drug protocol longer than most, with tolerable side effects. But these effects are cumulative, and eventually the body gives out. Of late I've been experiencing severe mouth sores. At first I thought rinsing with salt and water would relieve the problem. But with each rinse, the wounds got increasing worse. It hurt to eat and talk. I decided this was the perfect opportunity to attempt a stay-at-home retreat, with silence as a main objective.

I've been reading Dag Hammarskjöld. He writes: "The more faithfully you listen to the voice within you, the better you will hear what is sounding outside. . . . And only he who listens can speak." Further, "This is the starting point in the road towards the union of two dreams—clarity of mind to mirror life and purity of heart to mold it."

Today, the very idea of silence has become an oxymoron. Retreat centers are filling up with a new kind of pilgrim, who steals away from constantly hectic life for solitude. Silence is the most endangered quality of our time. Modern man strives for quiet.

But quiet, solitude, only happen in the here and now, and that can be unnerving. In trying to reconstruct something that is happening in the now, I often find myself confused and afraid. Only when I switch to that hard-to-reach, inner place do I become true to myself, wiser, and more willing to tell my story.

Sometimes I think I'm an anthropologist studying a primitive tribe and reporting what she finds with as much objectivity as possible. I'm, however, the subject of the study as well as its observer and analyst. Silence is the key to bridging the two. It enables each to be uniquely separate yet be bound together.

In silence, I can transcend my situation and gain precious insight that allows me to step beyond my reality—to shift my thinking, to observe, learn, and offer.

Body Image

Hair Today, Gone Tomorrow

It's a balmy summer evening in mid-August 2005. We are meeting friends for dinner and theater. Seven weeks have passed since my diagnosis. Harvey and I are the first to arrive at the recommended French place. I'm thinking about what to eat—French cuisine features more of the fats and creams my new digestion limits will not tolerate. I want to avoid an incident while I am in an uncontrolled environment; it's driving me crazy.

The ladies arrive. Both Jackie and Jenny rush over to me, arms extended to touch my full head of curls. Almost in unison, they exclaim how wonderful it is my treatment has not destroyed them. I am slightly put off, thinking how rude it is to focus on hair, as if that is what identifies me.

Yet as I sit and write this, thirteen months and three different treatment protocols later, I realize my journey regarding hair has led me into a dilemma of identity. Hair is not only about vanity. It is about dignity and, for me, a signature of who I am.

Having curly hair has always set me apart. As a toddler, my little face was framed with ringlets. They never needed to be fussed over. Each bath time included a little care in twirling strands of it around my mom's finger. Once set, the curls dried perfectly formed. Any activity, skipping or running, caused them to bounce. This, in the Fifties, led to comparisons to Shirley Temple. How lucky I was.

Attendance at the neighborhood Catholic grammar school created some problems: My curly head did not fit under the official school beret. The nuns made an exception, since there was no one else with such hair. Besides, those curls were a God-given gift. Several nuns, passing by my desk, had the habit of resting a hand on the top of my head as if to verify that my hair was real and, yes, that thick and shiny.

This distinction vanished with my teen years, when the fashion was bouffant flip. My mom refused to have my hair straightened. No meant no, and obedience to her was an absolute. Each night I doused my head with solutions to relax the curls and rolled the thick strands around rollers the size of beer cans. Sleeping was impossible, but the results were worth the lack of rest. Each morning I unrolled those rollers, and *voila!* My hair could be teased and sprayed into a very acceptable flip.

That is, until I walked outside. The weather could change my entire look—and attitude. Any moisture, the merest humidity, brought my curls back to life. As a result I wore my hair pulled into a slicked-back ponytail secured at the nape of my neck.

Once I began working, I joined the ranks of those who could attend a grown-up beauty salon. (Until then, my aunts had trimmed my hair.) At the salon I was able to cut off most of the curls. My objective to fit in, to be stylish, and curls, were not in vogue. I learned my healthy head of hair could take a cut and style if properly coaxed with magic potions.

The ensuing years were filled with life events in which my hair played a central role. Human Resources provided many opportunities to meet employees and make presentations to executives and their staffs. My reputation was solid and eventually preceded my arrival at the work site. When anybody asked who Rose Rappaport was, the usual response was, the "little one with the curly hair."

This identifier went unregistered, pushed to the recesses of my consciousness, until March of last year. Suddenly, after ten months of chemotherapy, my abundant mane was t-h-i-n-n-i-n-g. Each time I showered or combed it, my sink was covered with hair—not enough at first to alarm me, since I had so much of it, but when I could no longer braid it, the reality hit, and each morning brought floods of tears.... My dear friend David sat with me one day, looked me in the eye, and declared, "Rose, the human body will do what it needs to survive. Hair is dead tissue. Do you want to invest your attention and healing power on surviving cancer or on keeping your hair?"

The next day I called my hairdresser, Michael, who had been my friend and stylist for over twenty years. We made an appointment to visit two shops that specialized in "hair options" (I could not bring myself to talk about a *wig*).

At the first, we were greeted at the door by the owner, who looked like she needed a guitar and cowboy boots. Her taste in hair was something out of the Grand Old Opry. Michael took my hand, squeezed it, and began to ask questions. If nothing else, we would go to school and get educated about the world of wigs. During the next few hours I tried sundry lengths, shades of color, and styles. I learned that synthetic hair was easy to manage, less costly, and if styled properly, looked authentic. The base netting made a huge difference.

Throughout most of that episode, I could barely see clearly. My eyes were filled with tears. Suddenly Michael was thanking the owner, taking a card, and escorting me out the door. Back in the SUV, he told me we were going to his shop. Mondays the place was closed. It was eerie entering those silent, dimly lit premises stripped of their usual bustle. Michael said he should have thought of it before. Early in our relationship, he had cut my hair short. He would do so again. I had the face and stature for short hair. In half an hour, my limp, thinning locks had been transformed into a stylish do that framed my face. At that brief length, my curls came back. My head was certainly not as full as before, but I looked like *me*—even a younger version. This was not so bad.

This journey has provided me with special insights into the character of friends and family who have given me just the right advice about what to do next. Michael advised I should check out the other shop, just as an insurance policy. Better to have an option selected with hair on my head than be left guessing in the lurch.

Two weeks passed before I could make an appointment with Alexis. The one-on-one provided privacy: she specialized in clients with medical conditions resulting in hair loss. After she assessed my current do, she told me that I would not need a full wig, that she knew just the right color and style that would match my own curls. She would place an order and call me when it arrived. Two weeks later, back in front of her mirror, she cut the center from a full wig to create a hair piece that would enhance the top of my head. It blended nearly seamlessly with my own hair. She'd matched the curl in the pictures I had brought her. The hair piece had minute sewn-in hair clips to keep it in place. It looked great. I was so confident, I drove over to Michael's shop. It had been about six weeks since we had seen each other. He rushed over, kissed me, and exclaimed how pleased he was to see that my hair had grown in. The expert couldn't tell it was a hairpiece! I was elated.

That was February of this year. The new drugs worked fast, faster than I could ever have imagined. Of course my hair had changed during the past thirteen months, but the further thinning was dramatic—I could no longer clip the hairpiece securely in place. Each morning my pillow was filled with hair.

I felt cheated. I'd thought I had passed the hair challenge. It took a lot to call Alexis. She had saved the balance of the wig and would sew it together, restyle it. She would attempt to fit me in as soon as possible.

And so I wait. I am not interested in seeing friends or going out. I have come to think of these low points as entering the Pit. The Pit is that place of despair where I cannot see the light of day or any hope and only feel sorry for me. I have no other thoughts; I am frozen in sorrow. I just cry the sort of crying that takes your breath away, as when you hear an inconsolable child. The thing about the Pit is that it is dark and alone—the most horrible place your spirit or mind can enter. I have come to realize I hate being there. This may sound like not much of a revelation, but for me it was profound.

Most people would describe me as a people person—not a sickening sweet Pollyanna but (I would hope) an adult who enjoys being around people. I remember reading a remark once by Mae West. The interviewer was focusing on her carefree disposition and plain joy in living, and wanted to know about her philosophy of life. She straightened her back, smiled her coy smile, and explained that she did not want to surround herself with people who always agreed with her, but with interesting people who were curious about living and challenging themselves, people who could push the envelope and allow new ideas to be considered. At the time I thought, That's exactly the kind of people I want in my life: people who love debate, controversy, and the discovery of new ideas. Heaven forbid we all agreed. The Pit does not allow for interaction. It isolates and abandons.

Anyone with a life-threatening illness has known despair from the inside: the leaden inertia of the body, the global indifference to everything but the loss of well-being, the aversion to food, the urge to closet oneself away, the inability to sleep, the relentless grayness of the world.

When I hit the bottom of the Pit, I stay there until I can no longer stand me. I think, If I can't stand me, who will? And then I claw my way up into the light.

I am having a difficult time looking in the mirror. Up until now, no one could really tell I was sick. I did not look like a cancer patient. Although I had lost a fifth of my body, I am still at an appropriate weight for my height. My body never seemed this lean, and with working out each morning (I made a promise to myself that I would do all I could for as long as I was able), I looked good for a woman over fifty. I did not look like a skeleton, my skin color was adequate, and I had hair.

Proust wrote: "The real voyage of discovery consists, not in seeking new landscapes, but in having new eyes." And I am on an expedition to discover a new me—one who survives in the world, not just with the loss of curly hair, but without hair at all. I suppose, once I adjust to the idea of wigs as a permanent fashion accessory, I will begin to have fun with them. I really do not see myself as any other hair color than my own, but then, who can anticipate?

My next scan will not be for a few weeks. Until then I can only pray that this new drug protocol will be the one that affects me beneficially. My hope is that the life in my eyes and attitude will be what people remember when they meet me. I will not let hair define me or what my future will be. I will see myself with new eyes.

Naked Eyes

It has been several weeks since I have found the discipline to write. Topics in this series of essays are a matter of meaningful or noteworthy events but the determination is in the eye of this beholder.

When a person is diagnosed with a life-threatening illness, time and subject take on entirely different meanings. Time is slowed down so very much it sometimes feels you are walking through marshmallow. You move slowly, feel the stickiness, but when you look around its almost invisible. Subject selection becomes a matter of recognizing those aspects of living life that give me pause—a reflection on something I have not noticed before.

One such recognition occurred this week. Since my original diagnosis, my husband Harvey and I have tried to keep a "normal" life pattern. We rise at the same hour (almost), clean up, dress for the gym, and drive the ten minutes to the facility. The employees know who we are and always greet us with smiles and encouragement. Our workout usually consists of thirty minutes of cardio and a half-hour of weight training, a relic of our working days.

It started our day, got our motors going, and provided a sense of achievement—something for ourselves. It still does, and varies only when I have had a sleepless night or an early treatment. As I infuse every other Friday for an additional forty-eight hours, I rest and allow the power of the medicine to take hold.

This is not about exercise, however, but eyelashes. Frankly, I knew it was happening for a while. I look in the mirror each morning to wash my face and brush my teeth. But today it finally happened. I had *no eyelashes*. Unlike others who have lost their hair in one fell swoop, my hair loss has been gradual almost imperceptible, there one day and gone the next.

I leave the bathroom and begin to cry. Most women can identify one or two physical features they consider embody their beauty. For me they have always been my naturally curly hair and the length and thickness of my eyelashes. I feel my beauty is slowly being taken from me.

Harvey consoles my tears, speaking of inner beauty. In the scope of things, what impact does so small a strip of hair make?

They frame the eye, provide expression, and restrain the tears from streaming down the face. My eyes look naked. I suppose I could learn to attach false ones, but the thought of fussing with glue and strips of hair is unappealing. This may change, but for now I will look at the world through my naked eyes—perhaps to see a bit more clearly.

In Treatment

The Procedure

I ENTER THE BRIGHTLY LIT room. There are several young people mulling around the large CAT scan machine. This is the entourage of the primary physician, who will do the procedure. They all take turns to introducing themselves, and everyone assures me that what I'm about to under go is a snap. Easy for them to say. The scene is an operating room at Memorial Sloan Kettering Hospital. I am here for a nerve block. The pain in my back has increased over the last months. I have been on pain pills daily in addition to the ever-present pain patch. This block is usually reserved for patients suffering higher pain levels than me. My oncologist did not suggest it but is in favor of us moving forward. My husband Harvey searched the medical sites in an effort to find a way to reduce the amount of medicine I have been taking. The drugs are opiates and confuse me. Some would ask, "And how would we know the difference?" That's become the standard joke my husband

and I tell each other every time he speaks to me and gets this befuddled look in return. My concentration is shot. Reading is my life, and it has become unpleasant. I reread the same paragraph over and over with no mental digestion about the author's point or where I am in the story.

The block is simple enough. The patient is CAT-scanned face down, and needles are inserted into the lower back near the tumor. Alcohol is flushed in, deadening the site where the pain originates. Why is there pain in the back when the pancreas is in the abdomen area? The site of the organ is the Grand Central Station of the digestive, elimination, and cleansing functions of the entire body. In the middle of this bodily intersector, a tumor sits at the head of my pancreas. It is inoperable because it is adjacent to a major artery. The pain is indescribable and can bring me to tears in record-breaking speed. The meds to reduce the pain affect the entire region, along with brain functions. Sleep is one of the most common effects. I hate the reaction of sleeping my life away.

The anesthesiologist is my main focus. He will put me under, as opposed to giving me twilight sleep. As with any medical event, there are risks. There could be internal bleeding, a rupture of the blood vessels. Side effects almost always include degrees of nausea, diarrhea, and low blood pressure.

Given my present sense of fogginess, I accept the possible results and sign the paper. Harvey is about to leave. I kiss his face, make the sign of the cross, and lie face down on my stomach, pillows propping me up enough for the doctor to have a direct access to the site.

The next thing I know, I am in recovery. It continues to stun me how quickly time passes. All the television shows have led me to believe that they place an oxygen mask on your face, and you start to count backwards from 100. None of this is true. No sooner do they inject the drug into your IV than you are back in recovery.

Although everything appears to have gone smoothly, Dr. Cubert insists I stay the night. A room is a most precious commodity. We wait several hours. I have not eaten since dinner last evening. The monitoring nurse indicates a room may not be available until late into the night. Harvey decides to go home. We kiss, and I close my eyes to rest. It's about 8:45 p.m. before they locate a room. If they rush me to the seventeenth floor, I may just be able to order some food; otherwise, I must wait until breakfast the next morning.

Ann is the nurse on duty. As impersonal and sterile as the hospital setting can be, I have been intensely struck by the personal dedication shown by most of the caregivers. Not everyone is Marcus Welby or Florence Nightingale. But periodically you meet someone whose entire existence has been devoted to the care of patients they will likely never see again.

Ann makes me comfortable, explains the food ordering process, and checks my vitals. It appears my fundamental readings are something of a novelty. My resting pulse rate is 42, and my blood pressure is normally low. Considering my physical size and the fact that I work out daily, these are very coveted readings, but in a hospital filled with the infirm, they are dangerously low measurements. The stress on the cardiovascular system is enormous. The result is that my pressure will be monitored every half hour for the entire night. So much for sleeping. Dinner arrives, and I settle in. Around 11:00 p.m., another patient is brought into my room. She appears to have had surgery on her head, as she has been shaved in a strange pattern. During the night she calls out for ice packs for her head. We exchange greetings with a silent look that indicates we will listen and look out for each other during the quiet of the night.

The entourage returns to my bedside by at 6:45 the next morning. They ask how I spent the night and whether they can see where the needles were inserted. I explain about the blood pressure and ask when I will be released. They list the necessary activities I must perform before they will allow me to depart. They are in no particular order of importance...walking the floor, eating breakfast, going to the bathroom unassisted. I order breakfast.

Jackie, my roommate, has begun to stir. She shuffles to the bathroom. She is a young woman in her thirties. We exchange morning greetings, and she asks if we can have breakfast together. The rooms in this section of the hospital are set up like a hotel. You can order room service, and most likely you will leave sometime during the day. There is a moveable curtain that separates us at times when privacy is needed.

Jackie's husband works all day, so she will not have a visitor until late in the evening. We size each other up and decide it's safe to share stories. Jackie was born in Spain and has been in the U.S. for twelve years. She had a shunt placed in her head yesterday to relieve the pressure from the tumor that is growing there.

Up until our meeting, I thought *I* was the central figure in this essay, but Jackie is. You see, she was just diagnosed with a brain tumor. For the past seven months, she has had constant headaches, nausea, and vomiting. She was pregnant with her first child, a baby girl. The doctor wanted Jackie to take an MRI, but in light of the pregnancy, Jackie did not want to hurt the baby. Seven months passed before the last sonogram indicated that the baby's heart was no longer beating. Once Jackie had the miscarriage, an MRI revealed she had a brain tumor the size of a melon.

What do you say to someone who has just shared the most heart-wrenching story? We talk of survival, about how strong we Mediterranean women are and how blessed we are to have husbands who love us regardless of our appearance. Jackie continues speaking barely above a whisper. She knows she could not have taken care of the baby, that the loss of the child was for the best. Perhaps there will be another chance.

The release forms have been signed, and it's time for me to leave. I walk over to Jackie. We kiss and hold each other. I promise to tell others of her story and have people pray for her. She touches my cheek. We will never see each other again.

I am reminded of the saying, "I complained I had no shoes 'til I met a man with no feet."

I don't know how to end this essay. I have sat here all day and cried as I typed these words. Jackie is someone I will not forget, but more importantly, I hope *you* do not forget her—her love for her child, the courage to survive.

Don't Know What to Say

I AM RETURNING FROM a particularly long and difficult treatment. I sit in the passenger seat. We took the Porsche because it is easy to park. The stick shift is jolting, though; each twinge of pain is exaggerated. It certainly isn't Harvey's driving, it's my increasingly fragile body. I am sleepy. One of the drugs they gave me covers me in a mantle of sleepiness. They tell me sleep is beneficial as it dulls the conscious pain. I still hurt, only the intensity is pushed much deeper. Harvey tells me I moan during the night. I am unaware of the pain, but it remains. Occasionally a random lucid thought pushes through.

It strikes me that this is the perfect metaphor for the family and friends who have stopped calling. I know with certainty it isn't that they no longer care. They claim to Harvey, and themselves, that they don't know what to say—as if not speaking to me, not hearing the exhaustion and pain in my voice, negates the reality of the disease. It is then masked, pushed far enough down in their consciousness that the circumstance does not have to be dealt with.

I realize this is not about me but their own struggle with mortality.

The disease is just circumstance, the luck or bad luck of life. There was, and continues to be, no "reason" why it happened. But, mortality is the end result of living.

That sounds strange, but I have come to understand that each day since my diagnosis has been not about dying, but about *living*. Living to the fullest, in total awareness of the details that have so often gone unnoticed. Now they must be declared and recognized for their unique contribution to this planet and my life.

The Wave

MY MOTHER JUST CALLED. She is very upset because, for the last day and a half, I have not called. I usually talk to her every day. Mom is eighty-two and decides each day how I am by how I sound. When I sound chipper, then she knows I'm well. In an effort to spare her angst and worry, I play-act. I always try to sound upbeat.

It's been three weeks since the pain-blocking procedure. I have pain only on the right side below my rib cage and have been tender on and off for the last few weeks. Starting Wednesday, the intensity of the pain started coming in waves. At its peak, it brings tears to my eyes. On a scale of one to ten, it's a fifteen.

I call the pain center to describe the symptoms. The nurse, Angela, takes copious notes. I continue to take fewer opiates then other patients. Angela is pleasant enough, explains that pain management is just that—management of pain, not its total elimination. I know that pancreatic cancer is one of the most painful, and that I am doing very well. I listen politely, hang up the phone, and begin to cry.

Waves are a very appropriate metaphor for this pain. I visualize myself bobbing in the ocean. Up and down, up and down. The waves of pain bring me way down; sometimes to the point of drowning. The opiates neutralize my life. The more meds I require, the more I lose concentration. I sleep a lot, sometimes with my eyes wide open. The tradeoff continues to remain a major struggle.

When I am out of it, I don't return phone calls or go out. I enter the place of healing. The outside world, Mom included, does not understand the bobbing, the sense that, sometimes, when I am submerged in pain, the world and she do not exist. It is just me and the pain, and at times it dominates. The effort to "sound good" can take its toll. Lately I have an overwhelming need to stay true to me. I am so very tired of putting on a good face. The only person who knows the total truth of the reality of my days is Harvey. He is witness to hours spent stooped over in fetal position, moaning. No matter how recent the last scan or how positive a report from Dr. O'Reilly, pain drives me crazy. I search the internet. What organ is located on the right side? Is it low enough to be my appendix? Could it be my gall bladder? Of course it just could be the liver. After all, the liver is the processing factory for all that goes on in the body. Perhaps it, like me, is just plain tried of trying to process all the elements of this disease. The chemicals are harsh: Could they be taking their toll on my liver? I quickly reject the notion of going to the emergency room. At this stage, I feel I know more about what to do then they do. They almost always take an x-ray or order a scan to see what I feel. I know these pains are not in my lungs. They differ from the back pain I had several weeks back that led to the nerve block. I am frustrated and disappointed, yet I do know better than the experts. It's my body. I call, really, for reassurance that my cancer has decided not to advance. If I breathe into the pain and focus on the center, I am able to ride the wave. This provides some control. Like the surfer who is both exhilarated and scared, I am able to ride the wave for the moment. I will not take the opiates until I must, and for now I am riding free.

Scans

IT IS ONE WEEK after treatment. The pain in my ribs is constant; the only change is in degree. The burning in the pit of my stomach can only be described as a flaming hot poker searing my flesh. The antacids do not work fast enough. There is danger of over medicating. My oncologist has scheduled two scans. Heretofore, I have had a scan every eight to twelve weeks. The doctor is accelerating the timing. The actual scan takes minutes; the angst in my brain begins days before. Added to this worry are two additional scans, for bone cancer and blood clots

Neither my doctor nor I believe this to be a possibility, but all other efforts to alleviate this rib pain have met with little relief. I have been struggling to not hear the words in my innermost consciousness. I cannot even imagine what the confirmation would do to me. I challenge anyone to hear the words and not have a cold shiver run down your spine. It's the five-hundred-pound gorilla in the room. Neither my husband nor I talk about it. Sleep this week has been elusive. I medicate myself before I turn out the lights.

The pain and the burning return about 3:00 a.m. I shoot out of bed as the intensity starts at level ten and only goes up. Additional meds are not always practical. Attempting meditation as an alternative self-soothing takes time and concentration not always readily found. I attempt to say my rosary. The repetition of the Hail Mary distracts for a time. Rather than toss and turn, I slowly get up. It's now 4:00 a.m. I take my book, grab a throw blanket, and shuffle down the stairs. Sometimes sitting up and reading works. This week my trip downstairs has been filled with tears. Tears because the pain is relentless. Tears because I am frightened and the night is cold. Tears because I know I must travel much of this journey by myself. I pray for relief; the meds finally kick in; I fall asleep from exhaustion.

Resilience

I HAVE NOT SLEPT in two nights. The anticipation of seeing my oncologist is uppermost in my mind. We scheduled the scan two weeks ago, as the pain in my ribs continues to be bothersome. My brain refuses to turn off. I enter the dark cave of my mind more frequently.

Today's scan results are less than I expected. This is the third treatment protocol. Although the primary tumor remains constant, there is microscopic growth in the lesions on my lungs. Dr. O'Reilly does not express concern. We're in the eighteenth cycle of this drug protocol. The increase in size is not dramatic. Sometimes the cancer can be resistant to the treatments. This may be happening. The doctor assures me she has other arrows in her quiver. She is, however, holding off these newer drugs, since the side effects can be harsher. I listen carefully, wait for her to leave the treatment room, and begin to cry.

Early on in my diagnosis, my then oncologist Dr. Kortmansky

told us, patients know the results of their tests from how they are feeling. Could the fact that I am not sleeping be a sign of things to come? Everything has symbolism.

Family and friends have always remarked about my ability to accept challenges and figure out a way to approach viable solutions, execute action, stick to the plan. Why am I feeling so down? What the hell is the size of "microscopic"? Have I brought this on myself?

Dag Hammarskjold wrote: "Never look down to test the ground before taking our next step: Only he who keeps his eye fixed on the far horizon will find his right road." This sentiment mirrors my personal philosophy of "you create the world you live in." Heretofore, as a result, I have found the strength, the source of courage to surrender, to accept and put on a happy face. Today I am not so inclined. I infuse for one hour at the treatment center. I have taken the pre-cocktail mix to alleviate nausea and shakes. Laura, my assigned nurse, is attentive and senses I am off center. She is gentle as she wires me up. Like a suicide bomber, we attach the drug bottle to my port. This gives me the ability to infuse at home for an additional forty-eight hours. The drugs make me sleepy. I manage to crawl into bed. The sleep is welcome, dreamless. I don't remember how long I am away.

I awake with sorrowful thoughts. Harvey peeks into the bedroom to be sure I am OK. Can I share this overwhelming feeling in my heart? I am stumbling in the dark cave.

Sitting quietly, I attend to my inner voice, the one that wipes out the chatter and is the starting point of my spirit, allowing me to access clarity of mind, to see the mirror of my life and, in the depth of my heart, mold it anew.

It takes me some time to find this source: offspring of the past, pregnant thoughts of the future, clamor for my attention. It is the present moment, nevertheless, that always exists in eternity. At this point, time and timelessness offer a view of freedom. I enter the stillness.

I know the more I worry and fear, the larger it becomes, and the faster I sink, the harder it is to get out. Like attracts like.

In the cave, life looks harder. Everything feels more challenging—all because my inner self has gone from can-do openness to a murky place.

When I feel threatened, it's natural to hide until conditions are safe again. But pulling away, hiding within, removes me from the opportunity right in front of me—to interact with the situation and move through it.

Instead of running away, I must find the courage to stand and face my demons. They won't go away. They will just reappear in a different guise, usually more intensely. I need to absorb this news. I realize I have been here before.

Living thus far has taken its toll, and yet I would trade nothing. The richness and possibilities I can feel come directly from what I am experiencing. I am not there yet, but I do stand in awe of the transformative potential embodied in our consciousness.

I put on my slippers and shuffle down the stairs. Harvey looks up and smiles. For this, I continue the battle.

June 2, 2007

It's Saturday afternoon, and Harvey and I are comfortably mellow, watching the latest selection from Netflix. The doorbell rings; we look at each other, wondering who could be visiting. Harvey returns, carrying a lovely plant. The note is from our friends, Sharon and Kirk. "Thinking of you today with admiration and affection. Peace and Love." I burst out crying. Today, June 2, I begin my third year of survival. My reaction has been slowly simmering for days. My feelings are all over the map.

Anniversaries commemorate. Two years ago today was our first appointment with an oncologist. No one had used the dreaded "C" word, at least not directly. My seven-day hospital stay was surreal. The intermittent burning in my stomach had moved to a searing pain in my back. Previous doctor visits had resulted in stronger antacids and discussions about my "stress level". Dr. Gura, my GP, had had me on a liquid diet for three days. When it brought no relief, he'd decided to admit me to the hospital. It seemed liquid nourishment by mouth activates the digestive process, and he'd wanted to give the entire system a rest. The only way to do this was to place me on intravenous. The last time I had been in the hospital, fifty-two years before, I was six, having my tonsils removed. Now there were lots and lots of tests. Each day Dr. Gura stopped by to tell me that a different specialist would be conferring on my case. Suddenly I was a *case*. Memorial Day weekend came, and the last MRI would not be read until Tuesday. Dr. Gura sent me home with the promise to set up an appointment after the holiday.

That next visit totally changed our lives. Dr. Gura spoke in euphemisms—blockage, pancreas, Whipple procedure, the best surgeon at Sloan Kettering. These were the words I remember. We left the office shell-shocked. Were the words associated with *me?* Armed with all my x-rays, scans, and medical reports, we set up the first visit with the recommended surgeon. The entire experience was frustrating. He was very matter-of-fact. He did not like the scans we had brought and scheduled me to take an entire new series. This would take days to arrange. Our next visit was cancelled. Instead he called with his assessment. I was inoperable. The tumor involved an artery. He could not help me. The specter of cancer was becoming a reality.

Dr. Kortmansky was the oncologist assigned to my case. He discussed the findings and the recommended treatment schedule. Always a realist, I wanted the statistics. Given the site of the tumor and that it had metastasized to my abdomen and lungs, he said, this was Fourth Stage. The survival beyond a year was less than four percent.

A total out-of-body experience followed. Harvey and I held hands, looked at each other, and cried.

So why the mixed emotions? According to the statistics, I've beaten the odds. The longer I live, the better my chances of survival. I am in a unique club. Individuals diagnosed at the same time as me have long since succumbed.

I do lots of correct things to sustain my results. My support system is tremendous, my partner is unfaltering. My attitude most days is positive. Yet as I approached this anniversary, I have been further and further withdrawn. I don't want to talk to anyone. Sleeping has been a problem. I have been "in the pit." Usually I have to hit the bottom of the pit and walk around for several days. I grant myself permission to do so, but it doesn't usually last too long. I hate the pit and consider entry into it a total indulgence—my ability to climb out never a struggle. Now the walls are made of smooth, polished ice. Any progress I make to climb out results in little success. I keep slipping back, and as I fall I scream, *"Enough!"*—I want to be *me* again. I'm not just physically fatigued, my spirit is weary. I am tired of putting on a good face—of people saying the most inane things to cheer me up. I no longer want to be compared to "normal" folks.

These feelings have been brewing for awhile. Harvey is frustrated by my refusal to answer the phone or accept visitors. It is the first time I have expressed such wishes. I certainly don't intend to be mean spirited. I crave space and time, however, to be the me I used to be or at least pretend that I am. I don't believe I should have to explain why. Is that too much to ask?

Until

EVERY OTHER FRIDAY, WITH few exceptions, I have chemotherapy. At Sloan Kettering there is a routine. You sign in, spell your name, including any initials, and give your birth date. This is the first in a series of checks and counterchecks.

The chemo cocktail does not begin mixing until your vitals are taken—blood, weight, pressure, temperature. The phlebotomists know me after twenty-five months and usually comment on my outfit. The chatter is light. Taking blood samples from my veins has always been a challenge, but now I merely *see* the needle and my veins retract. They become invisible and hard to access. I can't look at the needle going into my arm—I've become needle phobic. The port in my chest can only be accessed by a licensed nurse. It is primarily for infusion of the harsh chemo drugs.

With this process complete, the waiting begins. Every other visit, I see Dr. O'Reilly, my oncologist, a pixie-like woman with the gentle touch of a true healer. She always has time for questions. She reviews vitals and authorizes the chemo to be mixed and administered. On alternate weeks this happens behind the scenes and we await our slot in the chemo queue. There are big bucks in cancer. The floor has a waterfall and comfortable couches; a variety of beverages and things to munch on are available. Orchids and exotic plants fill the tables. The waiting room is standing-room only. Most patients are on a prescribed cycle. Some stop to chat about their war story. Harvey and I sit quietly together. We don't want to hear others' plight. We have enough to deal with.

About an hour and half later we are called into the chemo suite. Marjorie, the majordomo, directs us to our station. Most cubicles have bright windows with plants. There are a recliner for the patient and chairs for visitors. A TV and VCR are available. Each cube is curtained off from the rest, making private conversation less than private. You can hear other people talking and nurses giving instructions.

Today, my attending nurse is again Laura, a bright, always smiling young woman from the Islands. She welcomes us and runs the checklist of side-effects. This week's has many more positive checks. While we were away last week, I had severe abdominal distress. This is code for lack of bowl control. I am sure there are worse indignities in the world, but for me it's one at the top of the list.

Laura checks all my blood vitals and notes my bilirubin is higher than usual. My olive skin tone does not show that I am jaundiced. Laura pulls my eyelid down and sees that the whites of my eyes are yellow. She calls Dr. O'Reilly, who immediately authorizes an ultrasound. As they suspect, the bile duct is blocked. This usually happens early on in the disease. It appears the main tumor is putting pressure on the duct, causing all sorts of distress. Dr. O'Reilly advises no chemo today and schedules a procedure immediately.

The weekend proceeds, with more yellow eyes and severe itching. The bowel distress continues keeping me close to home. I discover that, if I drink protein shakes and eat egg drop soup, my digestive system is eased. I do not sleep the night before the procedure. Dr. O'Reilly took all the blood work on Friday, so I am good to go.

The nurse on call describes the procedure and possible outcomes. I listen and think, *TMI*...too much information. Of course this is all necessary for legal purposes. No matter how much information they provide, no matter how many times they conduct the procedure, there is risk. I am afraid and hold Harvey's hand. He can't enter the operating room with me, so we kiss and I squeeze his hand, and off they wheel me.

The anesthesiologist describes what will happen. She is recommending full anesthesia rather than twilight sleep. It simplifies matters in case there is bile back flow. Before I close my eyes, I make the sign of the cross.

The next moment of consciousness, I am in the recovery room. My pressure always takes a long time to stabilize. Recovery takes three hours; then I am released. On the drive home, I am a bit in-and-out. My throat hurts, since they used a scope and camera down my esophagus. I take my antibiotics and sleep intermittently. My heartburn is back. This could be from lack of solid food. I pass an uncomfortable night.

The next morning I am up early. My entire body feels like it's been run over by a Mack truck. My neck must have been extended, along with my back and ribs. I hurt all over. I call the surgeon. His nurse calls back. The procedure was routine, she says; I should not be hurting. Dr. O'Reilly calls to check in. I tell her how I feel. This is atypical. She cancels this week's chemo and wants me to rest. I sleep most of the day. During the night, the pain spreads and I get worse. Harvey decides to take me to the Urgent Care unit, though I resist going—it's two o'clock in the morning. We arrive. The nurse takes blood, and I see the physician on call. Two things are unique to this procedure: no twilight sleep, and a new antibiotic. My complaints are unusual, but we decide together to stop the antibiotics. We enter the house at 5:30 a.m. I fall asleep. Stopping the antibiotic was the answer. The next day I am itchy, a symptomatic but delayed reaction. I recover but feel like a two-hundred-year-old man. The next few days I rest. My mother calls: she knows nothing of the preceding events, nor will she. I say I'm sorry to Harvey only a million times. He forbids me to say the word. It is what it is, and we are together. We sit on the couch, and he puts his arm around me. I am safe, until.

Family

Who Will Prevail?

My younger brother, John, has invited us to a barbecue. His son Jonathan is returning to college, and it's our family opportunity to wish him well. It's been a few weeks since Harvey and I have seen the family. I speak with my Mom and John daily.

Even with this frequency of contact, they have little understanding of my current pain level. This morning, activities revolve around which medicines to take; how fast they will take to kick in; how long they will be in effect. Does it make sense for us to venture out to this family event?

The arrival time is scheduled for 2:00 p.m.—that means that, according to family practice, eating, a major part of the gathering, won't happen until 5:00 or 6:00. Frankly, this is much too late for me. The pain on my right side continues to concern us. Harvey has searched the internet. The location seems to be the area of the liver and gall bladder. The ache comes in waves, at times very severe.

Breathing into the wave, surrendering to what's happening, works for the moment. Long term, it exhausts me.

I can see the wear on Harvey. We discuss like amateur chemists what could possibly work. I bring up the option of him attending alone. The answer: "*No way!*" Going and not feeling well is a waste. Disappointing the family is something I have not done since the start. Presenting a strong outward image saps my energy. The struggle does not seem worth it. I take a pain pill in the hope that it can remedy the current level of pain.

If I were a betting person, odds are I will attend and deal with the results later in the day. For me the key issue is living my life and not being controlled by the disease.

Today I am not sure which will prevail.

A Tale of Two Brothers

I SUPPOSE IT COULD have something to do with birth order. As the oldest and only female, life growing up in our first-generation Sicilian family was a real eye-opener to gender difference for me. My arrival was celebrated by every family member. But the euphoria of being the first didn't last long.

My grandmother used to tell the story that my mother would not let me cry—a fact I took full advantage of. I screamed and held my breath. In our two-family brick house, my novice mother ran down the two flights of stairs to my grandmother's apartment and hysterically claimed that I was going to die. Gram mounted the stairs slowly and deliberately, picked me up, and attempted to sooth me for a short time. When this failed, she laid me on the bed, turned to my mother, and said, "Let her scream. She'll catch her breath and calm down." Gram was always right.

I was a princess for just two and half years. My two talented aunts made all my clothes: Nothing was store bought. My full head of curly hair was something to behold—I was always being compared to Shirley Temple. I was a little star.

All that changed thirty months later when my little brother Carl was born. Although the second born, he was a *son*. The family name would continue. In European tradition, he outranked me a hundredfold. He had the body part I lacked.

Carl was an amazingly good baby. He always slept through the night. In fact, one time he slept fourteen full hours. Compared to the two-and-half-year-old screaming terror who insisted on her own way, Carl was a dream come true.

Things changed again when, nine years later, my brother John was born—cherubic, with a smile that seemed to encompass his entire face. I loved dolls, but here was a living, breathing one. I immediately took the role of surrogate mom. I volunteered to watch him every chance I got. I hoisted him onto my jutted-out hip, placed his arms around my neck, and off we went. The busybody neighbor across the street reprimanded my mother for allowing me to hold him in that way. It could injure my growing bones. My mother didn't listen, and neither did I. Instead of Patty Play Pal or Tiny Tears, I had John. I read stories to him, played with him, and comforted him when he was in distress.

I offer this backstory because, as adults, our relationships have fully blossomed in different ways. Interestingly, both my brothers work in Information Services. Both are analytical thinkers who can map complex business problems and distill practical, workable solutions. Carl's expertise is in executing, John's in business development. Both are smart but as different as night and day.

Because Carl was the first boy, he has always assumed the role of the older child. While we were growing up, my parents tended to rely on him. They sheltered me from distress because, after all, I was female. As a girl, my rules and restrictions could have filled volumes. When my friends were going out, my curfew was the earliest. As a young adult still living with my parents, I had to be home by 11:00 p.m., when most of my friends were just leaving for the dance clubs. I had a long list of house responsibilities—I needed to be trained to manage the housework for when I got married. Although I had the grades for college, my parents insisted I go to work immediately. Higher education was for the man of the house. I resented my brother Carl's status, and we never developed our relationship beyond the usual brother–sister spats. While he got away with murder, I remained a slave to the old world traditions of my gender.

My relationship with John continued to be close. Although he certainly was granted male privileges, he recognized my struggle for independence was paving the way for the family to fit into America. John was spared going to Catholic school. He attended co-ed public school and made friends with people of diverse backgrounds. He joined the drama club. His dancing partner, Kathy, was the first girl at our family dinner. In many ways he was breaking ground I could only imagine.

You may be wondering why I am writing about these relationships. I certainly know both my brothers love me—we share the same blood and traditions. Nostalgic memories tie brother and sister together with lives shaped by similar influences and experiences. Siblings relate to one another on many levels. I am attempting to grasp why their reactions to my diagnosis have been so very different.

John has been totally supportive. He calls every day, and not a month goes by that he does not take the time to come and see me. He is the only other person, besides my husband, who knows the depth of my pain and fears. We are able to talk about our view of the afterlife. John attends mass every day and has made a promise to fulfill First Friday devotions dedicated to me. He has walked each of the Fund Raising walks with us. He is there for me.

Carl, on the other hand, first came to see me a month after the initial diagnosis. As we prepared a simple lunch, I could tell from his expression that there was something on his mind. We only spoke about superficial things that afternoon. The next day we talked on the phone, and he declared I did not look sick and that John had misled him into thinking I was dying. Truthfully, I was taken aback. I told him I *was* dying, but so was he—that we were *all* dying, and that I was not *claiming* this disease—that I did not feel it was my time, and that I was not going to die of a diagnosis.

The next time I saw Carl, or his family, was at Christmas, almost six months later. Again he commented that I did not look sick. I suppose, in his way, that meant I looked good for a person diagnosed with cancer. There was no emotional investment or empathy—merely run-of-the-mill observation.

I have come to the conclusion that reactions of family and friends, and their behavior, toward my circumstance, are less about me and more about their own feelings of mortality—their beliefs in an afterlife their perspective on the mind–body connection. I have been saddened by Carl's apparent lack of interest. In one conversation he told me he could sympathize with me but could not empathize. My translations: He could feel sorry for me but could not understand. I hurt for a very long time.

Most recently, my eighty-three-year-old mom, never sick a day in her life, has been hospitalized for back problems. As is typical with the elderly, once in the hospital, the number of scans, MRIs and other medical tests will find something to be concerned about. We were fortunate to discover a large blood clot in her thigh. John is the closest in distance from Mom's house. He has taken on the role of primary caretaker. We confer on all matters, but the youngest has taken on the responsibility that, each for our own reasons, Carl and I cannot.

The other day we all happened to be visiting Mom at the same time. We kissed each other and teased, just as if we were all home in Mommy's house. I realized that, through all the years of misunderstandings, we have remained a family grounded in a history that keeps us humble. We know each other's tender spots, can say things to one another that one else can, and, hopefully show up in each other's lives at just the right time. I choose to believe this about both my brothers—that how a relationship weathers a storm is more insightful than how it sails on a sunny day.

Comments

It's a Sunday in May, and we have been invited to attend my cousin Sal's oldest girl's Communion celebration. In Catholic tradition, this is a seminal rite of passage. I remember my day and feeling something special and sacred about the entire event.

Today's festivities are being held on Long Island, and the little girls are dressed in long white dresses, resembling mini brides. Their average age is seven. Their hair and makeup are shockingly adult. The religious segment of the day is over before it begins. A big celebration is planned at a fancy nearby Italian restaurant. Sixty friends and family members have been invited. There is a DJ for the children. The entire atmosphere is circus-like and gaudy.

My younger brother, John, is bringing my eighty-three-year-old mother. I will see my aunt and uncle from Florida. I have bought a new dress and had my hair done. In retrospect, it strikes me as such a silly thing to do. There is not much hair to work with, but when Michael, my hairdresser for over twenty years, works his magic, my thin strands look fairly full. I am pleased with the overall effect, and Harvey has reassured me I can attend without wig or hat. I glance at the mirror one more time before we head out pleased with the results.

I sit next to my mother. My aunt is across the table. Mom turns to me and tells me I look very nice, but that she really likes my curly hair better. For a second I don't know what to say. I breathe deeply and tell her my hair will never be curly again, that the new growth is coming in straight and the texture fine. She stares at me and says, "You mean that's not a wig?" I'm rocked to my core. As if that were not enough of a blow, my aunt leans across the table and tells me she expected me to wear a wig and thought my hair was acceptable for what it was.

I stare at them. I am speechless. I turn to Harvey, who's sitting on my left, and tell him what has just happened. The confidence I had in the morning has vaporized. I am on the verge of tears.

Am I wrong to assume that family members could be more sensitive to my feelings? Do they think cancer has made me immune to inane comments? Is it a function of their age, this seemingly callous spewing of words that, if considered for the briefest of moments, would cause them to keep their comments to themselves?

It has taken me several days to deal with my feelings. The longer I consider my mother's words, the deeper I'm hurt. I suppose the reason there is a plethora of books, fiction and non, about mother–daughter relationships is the complexity. Mine has been no different. I am the only daughter and the first born in a first-generation Sicilian family; these are two huge reasons for drama. Sometimes when I reflect on memories of the past, I am amazed I turned out as balanced and rational as I am. But this is not about the past. It's about now.

When I was first diagnosed, Harvey and I told my brothers but not Mom. We did not want to upset her. But after much contemplation, I decided it wasn't fair to hold back the truth. Through her tears she continuously questioned how and why—two questions Harvey and I resolved rather quickly. It really did not matter how; the reality was the diagnosis. And the why? Well, truthfully, I have always felt this was just part of life and the cards I was dealt. There was no blame, no one to rant to, not even God. I did agonize for several months about what I had done to our life, Harvey's and mine. I could accept my fate, but felt extraordinarily guilty about the effect on our life together. But I digress.

In her accustomed care giving role, my mother immediately wanted to come, stay at our home, and "take care of me." It took many delicate conversations to persuade her this was not necessary, that, as long as I was able, I really wanted to continue to live my life as it has been. I could not imagine her living with us for any prolonged period, which would have been almost as bad as the diagnosis. That's an awful thing to say, but our relationship from the beginning always had conflicts. I was too independent, I read too much, I wanted to have friends sleep over. My dad, always a gentle man, rarely intervened. Any resistance to her rule was met with a turn in the hot seat, and I was most accustomed to that laser-like, focused place. My brothers fared differently—but, then, they were boys.

Our current relationship is generally a good one—age has moderated the war, and the battles have diminished with time. I call at least once a day, and we talk about whatever she wants. Lately she has taken to list a series of ailments that sound remarkably like the effects of my disease. She has a pain in her side, can't sleep at night, and even has gas. I have been in a quandary about why this annoys the hell out of me. At first I thought I was imagining it, but as I began to listen more intently I discovered that, whatever I said, the next day she had the same issues. Can these be sympathy pains? Since she can't take anything away from me, is this her way of sharing it? If this is the case, she is unconscious about what she is doing. I am more disturbed at why it bothers me. Is her need for love so neurotic, are her self-esteem and identity so low, that she can only relate to what others think and say about her?

Rather than confront the issue, I withdraw. I perform the obligatory calls, engage in the formulaic conversation, but keep my emotional distance. This is not my nature and feels badly, but getting sucked into her drama is detrimental to my well-being. Could this be the subject of a novel? I don't think our characters are interesting enough. I know I love my mom, and that, in her way, she loves me. It might not be the way I need to be loved, but is love nonetheless. And so it goes.

John

Harvey and I had just kissed good night and turned out the light. It had been a reflective day at our cottage in Nova Scotia. The micro climates of the area had ranged from heavy fog to brilliant sunlight.

I called Mom during the morning. The only other call was from my nephew Jonathan. He had just returned from six weeks' study in Italy. Although I received detailed bulletins from my brother John, hearing Jonathan's happy voice was a special treat. It was early afternoon, and he was about to join his buddies for a quick game of basketball. He and the family planned to go see the new Harry Potter film that evening. Life was good.

At 11:30 p.m. the phone rang. Calls in the middle of the night are to be dreaded. It was Jonathan, telling me he'd never thought he would be making this call. I knew in an instant it was about my brother John. The words I remember are *massive heart attack, they did everything they could*. John was gone.

What can I say? How do I capture a life in an essay? I can't say his name or think about him without crying. I only hope to reflect a tiny fraction of John's brilliant spirit in the telling of stories.

Mom would say John and I were twins nine years apart. We thought and acted as one. We were kindred spirits. As a child I held him in my arms and played with him. Our bond was beyond that of a normal brother–sister relationship. We spoke everyday about everything. Our intimacy was always leavened with respect and trust. Before this most recent trip to Nova Scotia, I told him not to call every day, that telephoning was costly. John simply said, "Ro, I like talking to you, and when we don't, I feel something is missing from the day."

John was the primary caretaker of our mom. Although she lived alone in a retirement community, he stopped by each morning on the way to work. He dropped off the newspapers, checked to make sure she had spent a comfortable night, and headed off to work. He managed her financial and medical affairs. We discussed all the details, alerting each other with our own observations about mom's behavior. In the family, John was the go-to person, his personality light and energized. He went to daily mass. With news of my illness, his dedication to our relationship intensified. Although he traveled extensively for work, he managed to visit me at least every other week. We both shared our struggles of living our Catholic faith in a world not always conducive to its values. We discussed how Christian behaviors could be interpreted as weak in the business world, that understanding the political scene was important. John would listen thoughtfully and then tell me, "But, Ro, if God is on my side who can hurt me?"

Although I debated the fact that, when the Lord walked the earth, He'd thrown the money changers out of the temple, I would smile and shake my head. Of course John had the better answer.

In our quiet moments together, John and I discussed how I wanted my funeral to be conducted. Because of these conversations, I knew what John wanted for his. The operative word was simple—a celebration of a life. Who would have thought this irony of circumstance would be turned.

Over a thousand people came to the viewing. They lined up around the block. The funeral director kept coming in to tell MaryJean, John's wife, and Jonathan to move the line faster. But it seemed everyone had a story about John. You see, John didn't have a special relationship just with me; he shared his joy of living with everyone he came in contact with. The last thing I want is for you to think that John was a preacher. He simply lived his life. An electrical engineer by education, he had his doctorate from Polytechnic University. He was an executive in business development with a telecommunications company. Although the company had transferred ownership many times, John remained a constant. He was respected and liked. Little did we know how much. Even security guards came to pay respects. They knew John because, each morning and night, he'd greeted them by name, brought them donuts when no one else seemed to see them.

Mood

Work

IT MAY SOUND SILLY, but this week I applied for a job. Even though my last corporate position was five years ago, I still receive notices from several human resource networking groups about opportunities. Periodically, I wonder about bothering with these emails and consider taking myself off the lists. But in some bizarre way I feel they keep me connected to my career.

The feelings associated with giving up something loved—or at least something that was a part of me for most of my adult life—include doubts about self-worth. As much as I always thought my job did not define me, it did. I had a title, the respect of others, a more than adequate paycheck. Life had a consistency. Routine provides a comfortable sense of belonging. Certainly not every day was bliss. The higher the levels achieved, the more the responsibilities, the more quirky personalities and stress come your way.

Some aspects of the workplace have lost their importance, and I can give them up easily. Others, the social and collegial, are difficult to replace. Loneliness can be a major factor in chronic illness. Days can become endless, and the significance of daily activities less worthy than the tasks of the workplace. Applying for this position means I still have something of value to contribute.

I applied for a part-time HR slot in Elmwood Park, about a twenty-minute car ride on Route 80. They asked for someone with three to five years experience. My letter of application requests they not discount my twenty-plus-year career, that I have been doing consulting and miss the sense of community a staff job provides. I attach my resume with my letter of introduction and hope for a positive outcome.

Work is a great anesthetic when you are dealing with illness. I am one of the lucky ones who does not look like a typical cancer patient. My weight is usual for someone my height and has been steady; my hair has begun to grow back, although its texture is thin and straight. So I pass for healthy.

It's my energy and stamina that are in question. Treatment causes a constant struggle over how to establish activity limits so I am not overextended or stressed. I have to worry about boundaries, because chemotherapy has taken away any reservoir I could have hoped to tap into.

My application makes me wonder how I would respond to interview questions. How will I explain my every-other-week treatment schedule? If it's a part-time position, do I *have* to reveal this? What if people at work find out? A stigma attaches to those with cancer who continue to work. They are either pitied or feared. Their presence reminds others of their own mortality. You become a symbol of their fear, and of how much life is about loss. This is an interesting experiment. I would like to see how far I can progress with it. I always have a choice. But then, don't we all?

Bubbles

EARLY IN OUR MARRIAGE, Harvey and I discovered a mutual passion for the theater. We love the whole thing, from dressing up (we still do) to the fancy dinners and audience chatter that turns to silence when the curtain goes up. Of late, we only go when discounted tickets are available: it has gotten quite expensive. As a result of the internet, we are listed with several discount services and receive many offers via email for both Broadway and off-Broadway fare.

The last few shows we have seen starred Hollywood actors in short-run, somber, classical works. The latest was *A Year of Magical Thinking*, with Vanessa Redgrave, from a book by Joan Didion, who describes her grief in the year in which she lost both her spouse and creative partner, John Gregory Dunne, and her only child, Quintana, at the age of thirty-nine. She described how she lost her mind, her logical thinking. The book was her salvation and re-entry into the rational world.

After seeing this play, I turned to Harvey and told him, "No more serious subjects." Now, sometimes I say things in the moment and forget I said them. This seems to be happening more these days.

I'm not sure if its age or the quantity of drugs I take.

It was no wonder, in any case, when Harvey subsequently told me we were going to see an off-Broadway performance artist whose show was entitled *A Gazillion Bubbles*.

My adult experience with "bubbles" had been restricted to the recent economic bubble in the real estate market and the dot-com start-ups. Both, although attractive at first, burst into quite a sloppy mess. You can understand why my first reaction was, How very silly, but the tickets had been bought and we were going.

We entered the theater and found an entire audience filled with stressed-out parents and hundreds of eager children ranging in age from three to about twelve. We settled in and within minutes were mesmerized by Fan Yang, a Vietnamese-Hungarian. He has laid claim to twelve *Guinness Book* records for bubble making. His work was fascinating, and we soon got caught up in it. There were bubbles within bubbles, gigantic bubbles that enveloped ten people, bubbles in laser lights. Fan Yang selected volunteers from the audience, and the kids were great—really into the drama and magic. At one point the entire theater was indeed filled with gazillions of bubbles.

Suddenly I found myself crying without knowing why. Harvey looked at me and asked if I was in pain. I shook my head. These were not tears of sadness but joy. I realized I was feeling sheer bliss. As adults, we rarely allow ourselves to connect with the child within. There was no hidden meaning to the performance but a release of emotions that was not merely cathartic but profoundly calming.

Given the past twenty-one months of doctors and scans, medicines and pain, it was a soothing balm for a weary spirit. We left the theater with enormous smiles and a promise to look at the simpler things in life—like bubbles—for the joy they bring.

A Gift

I HAVE ALWAYS BEEN a self-reflective person and up to now have thought this inclination a blessing. Now it seems I'm incapable of turning it off, or even quieting the chatter. Over the last twenty-three months, my inner witness has taken stage front and center. At first I thought that taking a writing course would allow the noise to quiet down—that the act of writing would assist in emptying my mind so I could rest. Not so. I decided from the onset that I had choices regarding how I would manage the balance of my life. I now know that this idea of choice is really the only way I know. I am compelled to behave so. The insights I have gained, and the appreciation of simpler things have shown me that, in some bizarre way, this period of my life has been a gift.

According to *Webster's Unabridged*, the word *gift* means: "that which is given or bestowed; anything which is voluntarily transferred by one person to another without compensation or donation; a present."

That sounds incongruent. How can a diagnosis of pancreatic

cancer be a gift? But it has been. Now let me be clear: Were God to sit me down and present me with a basketful of "gifts," this would not be one I chose. Two years ago I'd have run away from it. People build walls around the sick. They project onto them their own lack of hope. They can deny their own death by portraying dying people as essentially different.

That's how I thought two years ago. But the dying are part of the living. Today I am more inclined to step out of my comfort zone. Hell, *cancer* is out of my comfort zone. Today I try new things, think more boldly, even consider that these essays may be worthy of others' interest.

I have come to think of this gift I've received as a package with a stone in it. The outside is wrapped plainly. At first, when I open the present, I am disappointed. The stone is heavy and dark. But I pick it up and begin to examine it. I finger the surface and realize there are many facets to its texture. As I study each, I learn something new about the gift—and more importantly, about me.

One of those facets is surprise. Like most couples, Harvey and I had plans for our future. We have learned that anyone who thinks they're on top of things and has life all figured out must either be really unaware or asleep. Uncertainty, unaccounted for encounters with the novel, are inherent in living, and no assortment of retirement homes and IRAs, no bank balance or stock portfolio however large, can nullify them.

That includes dying, of course. We are all moving through time, which means each and every one of us must face certain death as well as try to unravel the daily mystery of the unknown that is life.

I have learned, for example, that my sense of who I am, my identity, requires others. I cannot be me without this. I need to be seen and heard, and not rendered invisible by the mantle of cancer. The need is more compelling now than ever before. I must record the story, the awareness. I hope to provide not just a roadmap for how to get through a life-threatening illness, but insights and discoveries that lead to a full, vibrantly active life. I imagine that I am something of an advanced explorer sending a map back to others, a catalogue of the secrets hidden in everyday activities—that are so obvious we ignore them. Living with this disease has thus far certainly been an occasion of creativity expansion and cause for daily celebration. To be completely human is to commit ourselves to what we do not fully know, yet venture forth with an open mind and heart to discover something new each day.

This understanding should alert us to our delusions of grandeur, awaken us from the false belief that we can escape suffering and death, and counter the pervasive lie that we are superior to other humans beings and capable of escape.

That Which Cannot Be Named

I PROMISED MYSELF THAT I would write essays about the realities of pancreatic cancer—those conditions and issues that affect living a healthy normal life. So why such a strange title? The phrase appears in the popular series about the boy wizard Harry Potter. 'He who cannot be named' is the boy's nemesis. The ongoing battle between the two peaks and swirls, with Harry not always at the advantage.

The image strikes me as the perfect one for my dilemma. The condition I am attempting to manage is. . .well, it goes by several names. Those that come to mind bring the laughter of little boys watching the British comedian Benny Hill. Breaking wind, gas, the toots, flatulence or as my mom delicately phrased it when we were children, "bunnies"

The pancreas is one of the organs in the digestive system. Its primary contribution is to help digest fats. All the organs perform a well-orchestrated ballet when functioning optimally. Just one minor imbalance and the entire process goes awry.

As I've progressed through this diagnosis, I have attempted to view each challenge as a massive experiment. I am part Colombo and part mad scientist, combining or eliminating potential elements that create the dreaded enemy—gas. There seems to be no rhyme or reason to what works or doesn't. Because my innards have a mind of their own, I cannot estimate processing times. Prescribed enzymes that are supposed to replace what my pancreas isn't producing add more complexity to the mystery.

My petite body produces Jurassic amounts of pent-up air. The bloating distends my abdomen to a new pant size. The pain can be excruciating. It feels like I am about to pass a stone the size of Gibraltar. Pain, however, is the least of my problems. The doctor cannot tell me why, but the smell can only be compared to that of a large dead skunk. Over-the-counter remedies only expel this built-up air for what appear longer periods of time. I've tried various foods solo or in combination with the intensity of a master chef. Sometimes the resulting effects are immediate; sometimes they take hours; all the time, it is just plain embarrassing.

I've taken to not eating before events. The risk of bombing the place out is too humiliating. I cannot tell you how many movie scenes I have missed with a mad dash from my chosen seat. Suddenly I vanish in my attempt to spare others nose-wrinkling and eye-watering expressions. Sometimes the gas escapes quickly, before I can make haste. Of course I have noticed the reaction of my nearest neighbors. First there is a wave of the hand, then nervous looking around with a panicked glance—to ensure those in the immediate vicinity that this rudeness did not emit from them. My acting skills have been honed during these occasions. I continue to stare ahead, not noticing or smelling anything. (Aha, if only that were true. I die a thousand times.)

And like Harry Potter, who does not know why this enemy has chosen him, I realize the malordous problem is just one more lesson to live with.

Just What Is Hope?

MANY WOULD SAY THE line from Dante's *Inferno*, "Abandon hope, all you who enter here," is an opening mantra for anyone diagnosed with cancer.

Some physicians, in their desire to provide honest expectations, offer gloomy prognostications. As a realist, I want the truth, which is not the same thing. After twenty-six months, I have come to the conclusion that physicians should be ministers of hope and comfort to the sick. The statistics of life expectancy hinge on so many variables—the patient's overall health, family medical history, individual reactions to treatments, their financial and people support systems, personal life philosophy, and belief in a higher power.

Being ill is bad enough; being hopelessly ill is beyond what any human being is meant to endure. One can't hope for what has already happened. Hope has nothing whatsoever to do with prognosis. It is an interesting emotion, a very complex desire modulated by belief, not impulsive but characterized in thoughtful intention. Faith requires imagination—not fantasy, but the apprehension of the as-yet unrealized. It depends on one's belief that an uncertain future good one desires may possibly happen. In other words, hope depends on an act of faith. Hope has an apparent future. The machinery has everything to do with the human spirit. It is a dimension of the soul.

Pain

Jellyfish

It is May 2006. We are walking the beach in South Carolina. My friend Bob has provided his beach front condo for a week.

This is a major accomplishment.

Back pain has kept me awake most of the time we have been here, the intensity of it a new experience. Since my diagnosis last June, I have experienced little pain, and its depth and suddenness frighten me. It begins with severe heartburn and immediately moves to level-ten back torture. Each morning we hold hands and walk the entire stretch of beach. I am almost fully clothed (exposure to the sun is a no-no).

This morning the tide has washed up hundreds of jellyfish. I stop to watch. It occurs to me that's what this pain is all about. Like the jellyfish swept up by the ocean to lie on the shore awaiting the next wave to rescue it and return it to the world it knows, pain takes me from my comfort zone to a place where I sit and wait for the relentlessness to stop.

Ice Water

THE LAST TEN WEEKS have been saturated in an onslaught of medical issues. I have not picked up a pen for the entire duration.

As I reflect on this time, I realize I have been enveloped in a fog of new challenges. Instead of playing checkers, we are learning the rules of three-dimensional chess. The quality of our life has shifted dramatically. I have no intention of boring the reader with whining words of self-pity. Yet I feel compelled to describe the key elements in this shift of focus.

In the middle of the night on July 14, we were awakened by a call no one wants to receive. My nephew Jonathan called to tell us my youngest brother John had died of a sudden and massive heart attack. John would have been fifty on August 23. Details of his life and death, of our extraordinary connection, deserve an essay of their own—one I am incapable of writing at this time. His loss has, in any case, affected my entire belief system. The psychological term is *survivor guilt*. I am not angry at God but just very confused. Suffice to say

I have been inconsolable. Such grief, of course, has an effect on the mind and body.

The week of John's wake, I also received the results of my latest scan—none of it uplifting. The rib pain I have been complaining about for the past year finally was revealed as cancer. Sometimes the patient will feel what is happening at a microscopic level long before the doctors can see it. Without visual evidence, treatment cannot be administered. Dr. O'Reilly was optimistic about the prescribed treatment: ten days of targeted radiation, carefully mapped out since the cancer was very close to my lung. The other news was that, although the cancer remained contained in the original site, new cells were coalescing in my abdomen and lung.

Whenever Harvey and I receive sad news, our reaction is silent tears. We both need time to integrate what the information means. Frankly, my thoughts draw me to John and the relief joining him would bring. I am exhausted mentally and physically by the news. I disclose none of this to Harvey. We discuss plans to visit our Nova Scotia home for our twenty-ninth wedding anniversary and agree to begin the radiation treatment when we return.

I force myself to have happy thoughts of sharing ten glorious days on the Bay of Fundy, reveling in the scenery and sunsets.

This was not to be the case We drove all day Sunday, ten hours, to Maine so we could take the ferry from Bar Harbor on Monday morning. But since we enjoy each other's company and had several new jazz CDs to listen to, we settled into our journey. Despite travel exhaustion we had a lovely dinner at a stunning restaurant on the Maine coast. I watched people eat, as I really cannot eat too much. It's interesting to me the things we pay attention to once they are denied us. I saw an elderly couple devouring some pretty hefty lobsters. My grilled, dry salmon hardly satisfied my taste, but I did enjoy watching the enthusiasm and gusto of the scene before me. We took a short walk after dinner and made the 8:00 a.m. ferry with ease the next morning.

By the time we reached the cottage, I was not feeling well. My level of tiredness did not match the previous day's activities. That Monday night a new medical adventure began.

Harvey knows I would never wake him up in the middle of the night if it was not serious. I was having trouble breathing. My lungs sounded congested, and I could not catch my breath. I was scared. Although he wanted to take me to the local hospital, I insisted on rest. This decision, I believe, saved my life. Harvey held me, and eventually we fell asleep. The next day, I lingered in bed most of the day. Although this is not my usual habit, I again felt I needed to rest. Tuesday night; my breathing was better but not back to normal. Wednesday, I stayed at home, and Harvey did errands on his own. I called my oncologist. Erica, Dr. O'Reilly's nurse, listened to my description and wanted me to check into the hospital.

The local hospitals are small, and a trip to Halifax was two hours away. I promised I would check the ferry schedule and call her back. It would take a full day to get back to the States. I set an appointment with Dr. O'Reilly for Friday.

We were fortunate enough to obtain a Thursday reservation on the ferry and drove through the night. With little sleep, we made it to our morning appointment with the doctor. After one listen to my chest, the doctor immediately sent me for scans. I had all the classic signs of a pulmonary embolism—a major blood clot in the main blood vessel of my right lung. We were immediately put in an ambulance and deposited in the Sloan-Kettering ER. I stayed hospitalized for five days. We were in shock through most of it. In the middle of the drama, we were asked to reconfirm my DNR (Do Not Resuscitate) order. If the reality of my condition had not otherwise been apparent, signing that form was like ice water in my face.

The upshot is, yet another medicine. I must now give myself a daily injection of blood thinner in my abdomen. This will not dissolve the current clot, but it will avoid the development of future ones.

Because of the location, my breathing has been compromised even further. Walking the simple flight of stairs to our bedroom is like climbing Mount Everest. I no longer can play-act that life is just fine. The slightest stress or aggravation causes me to have labored breath. I have curtailed discussions with my mother, which aggravate me. Her lack of understanding and denial of my circumstance are not my problem. I understand this now, and the emotional engagement has diminished.

The disease has entered a new phase. As it becomes more complex, my medical options have lessened. After all, I have beaten the survival odds for more than twenty-six months. Although my behavior may not demonstrate it, writing continues to be important to me. The high level of opiates clouds my concentration. My grief hinders my attention. I find myself sitting and crying. My ability to get out of neutral is difficult. I hope my intention to resume writing shifts my current state. I must try.

Love

A Dream Come True

It's a mid-June Saturday night; Harvey and I are holding hands watching the sun set over the Bay of Fundy.

We purchased this cottage last August, months after my diagnosis. The decision filled me with mixed emotions. How often would we be able to travel, given my treatment schedule? Would there be time to create memories? Harvey listened to my fears, took my face in his hands, and said, "If we share it for just one day, it's a dream come true."

For two individuals born and raised in New York, we pinch ourselves to make sure we are not dreaming. One of our favorite dates always was to pack a lunch, drive out to the beach and enjoy the rhythms of the shore. You may wonder, why Nova Scotia? More relevant, where *is* Nova Scotia? It is a peninsula on the Atlantic coast of Canada, just north of Maine. It has temperate weather most of the year and less snowfall than Boston or New York. Our cottage is on the bay, in the middle of five acres of forest; and the big picture windows, which face west, capture the most amazing sunsets we have ever witnessed.

As we neared retirement and visited our relocated friends, we explored the purchase of a home near water—financially prohibitive in the United States. Affordable communities usually consist of multiplex high rises with some ocean view. We almost gave up the dream until we discovered Nova Scotia on the Internet. Realizing downloaded pictures can be deceiving, we began to vacation in towns we thought might be to our taste. The bed-and-breakfasts provided insights into the areas. We fell in love with the scenery and the less complex lifestyle.

Rachel Carson has a wonderful line about the seashore which she calls "a place of unrest, of dual natures wet and dry—old as the earth but never exactly the same from one tide to the next."

I have been mesmerized for as long as I can remember by the sigh of the tide, breathing in and out of the shoreline—forever and ever. Now when I stare at the horizon, at its emptiness, at the straight line between sea and sky, its expanse puts everything into perspective.

As the sun melts into the horizon, the overhead sky is cerulean, nearly purple, like blue chocolate, smooth. The beach is sculptured with black rocks. They have existed for eons, watching the fishing boats lay lobster traps. The landscape, and my perspective, combine to tell me this place is special, sanctified. For me it provides fullness to the hunger for escape, a respite from the reality of cancer. It satisfies like nowhere else.

Out here I can hear the rhythmic hum of near silence. If I listen close enough there's even music in the grass.

Intimacy

Love—influenced by Hollywood and Valentine's Day sentiments—is one of the most overused and underappreciated words in our language. So is *sex*. Given the fact that our society has fewer boundaries than ever before, it's interesting that the latter is difficult for anyone to talk about. With the plethora of information on theory, techniques, and reactions, you would think we could be in touch with our own specialness, with what it takes to make individuals come together and become one. There is *so* much more to sexual intimacy than a lower body explosion. The sexual experience can occur without loving or being "in love." Consider our ancestors, who were married off in early youth to partners chosen by their parents on grounds that had nothing to do with love. They went to the act with plain animal desire. But love in its deepest sense is far more complex still, far more than a network of romantic impulses.

Illness complicates this picture even further.

With illness, sex involves endless physical constraints. A lot depends on how I am feeling. Have I slept the night before? Is the pain in my ribs too great? Is either of us preoccupied?

When we lie down together, almost always we pass through a moment of tension. Who will make a move first? Will either of us turn away just because we are too tired? In over thirty years, we have established a code. We judge the moment and ask, "Do you want to be with me?" These words mean so much more than physically being together—our intimacy transcends the obvious.

As I reflect on these differences, I fall into the very issue. How do I write about our love, Harvey's and mine, and honor the experience with dignity and uniqueness? Do I dare attempt to express my feelings? Love songs only touch the surface

How do we *live* in intimacy? By holding on and letting go. Intimacy demands that we cleave to one another, commit ourselves to the hard work of listening and adjusting our own desires. Intimacy knows the details of each other's lives: what makes us smile, what we fear, what we like in our tea.

St. Paul (1 Corinthians 13:6) says: "Love rejoices in truth." When we know the truth of another's life, and more importantly when we know the truth about ourselves, we share intimacy. This truth seeking is not easy to achieve. It requires a vulnerability and exposure that normally lie hidden in the recesses of our ego. It's less about how we physically look and more about who we truly are. We must preserve this naked truth—the truth we share with each other—if life is to be complete.

We need to recognize something greater than ourselves—that there is something beyond words, beyond behavior. We must be willing to step over the apparent, cross into mystery—believing in the power of love.

At night, when pain is too great to describe, when drugs are not relieving it and my mind is too scared to function, Harvey turns to me, puts his hand on the place of the pain, and tells me to breathe into it. After awhile, my breathing is shallow no longer; our breath, our heartbeat, become one. In that moment of mystery, the fear lifts. I am no longer alone; we become one, and he allows me to relax enough to enter a zone of no pain, of peace, of total love.

The latest scan finally indicates what we have suspected for a while. The pain in my ribs shows the cancer is in my bones. We are scheduled to see the radiologist. More troublesome are the lesions in my lungs, which increasingly steal my breath.

Cancer is not for the faint of heart when it comes to intimacy. There are no words to say. Our silence screams the reality of the inevitable. I watch Harvey watch me. I wonder how many more times we will make love. My heart is heavy with so much longing. I keep thinking that although our lives have been blessed in so many ways, forever is not enough.

Anniversary

THE WEEK HAS BEEN a roller coaster of emotions filled with good and bad surprises.

Friday I had normal treatment. Katharine wired me up for two days of at-home infusion. Thank God, Harvey knows how to disconnectthe tubes taped to my chest. Sunday morning we disconnected and looked at each other.

We kiss. Today is a *gift* in a very special way. We are married twenty-nine years.

I reflect on this time last year. The diagnosis was proclaimed in early June. Our August anniversary was filled with tears, our minds reeling with thoughts of the unknown and common facts found on the internet. It could have been our last anniversary together. We clung to each other most of the day. But that was then, and what a difference a year can make. Although the reality of the disease is truer, the tubes taped to my chest quite real, and feelings of nausea dominate the next two days, yet we are looking forward to the future.

Before the diagnosis we discovered the beauty of Nova Scotia. We found a charming town in the Annapolis valley region. We have managed to visit during each season. Each time we described how much we would love to have a cottage, family and friends gave us a look that clearly indicated they thought we were crazy. Contrary to all their opinions, we are traveling there to close on a home in Young's Cove.

From the earliest days of our marriage, we have dreamed of a home with a water view—a place to relax and listen to the sounds of the sea. Friends who have retired have moved to other parts of the U.S. We have visited each location in the hope that it was the place for us. None possessed the feeling and sunsets of Annapolis Royal. Each of our visits included some house hunting, each time a bit more aggressively. We even bid on a home last year pre-diagnosis, but the deal fell apart. Little did we realize that fate was working. Our cottage is directly on the Bay of Fundy, on five acres of forest with 375 feet of waterfront. This house is positioned to take full advantage of the sunsets. We wake up to watch the sun illuminate the horizon in shades of pink and powder blue.

Reading this, you may wonder how smart a decision this was. After all, I have treatment every other week, the distance is long, and we still face the reality of pancreatic cancer. We are realists, however, and no matter the time, this is a dream we can fulfill for as long as we can.

This decision has energized me. It demands plans for the future, new memories to create and share. We are living a dream and feel blessed to achieve it.

Life is about change, flux, when the future is a blank sheet of paper waiting for you to write on it. The strength to live with uncertainty in a new wilderness, in the face of death, translates to what I call faith.

Soulmates

I AM QUIETLY SIPPING a cup of herbal tea as I recover from a particularly painful night. I'm thinking, not about me, but about what goes on in the mind and heart of my husband Harvey.

We have been together for twenty-nine married years, plus four years of courtship. Ours has been an uncommonly loving relationship. We can complete each other's sentences, with a glance know what the other is thinking. We are still crazy about each other, and most importantly, he can still make me laugh. We cried our tears and held each other with the first news of the diagnosis. Ours is not a sad life but a celebration of its gifts.

We have traveled to Tanzania and Beijing, shared losses of jobs, difficult bosses, family conflicts, and the departure of loved ones. Our love has been quietly strong. We still hold hands and kiss upon waking and turning out the lights. We are soulmates—different enough in our thinking, feelings, and behaviors to still surprise each other, keeping us individually curious about the other.

Selfishly, I have only recently begun to think about what is going through his mind. He cannot take away the pain or the reality of my diagnosis. Sometimes I catch him looking at me as if he is attempting to etch my image in his mind. He holds me when the pain is too much, his voice urging me to breathe into the intensity, to surrender to the waves. We have talked about what happens after. How I really do not want him to become a recluse. How the memorial service should be designed, how much our love has meant to each other. We spend most of our days being together, cherishing the time we have for however long, celebrating the days I feel good and holding each other when I don't.

He is my heart, and it is his love that keeps me strong, willing to try yet another new drug or procedure. Believe me, it would be much easier to despair, to take enough pain medicine to sleep all day. I do not want to leave him. This was not part of our life plan, yet we are stronger because of it. Together we are invincible; together we hope.

Connections

My Friend Albert

YESTERDAY I ATTENDED THE funeral mass of Al Boggiano. I met Albert, or should I say Al met me, at daily mass. It was October 2001. 9/11 had changed the world but also my immediate life. The position I loved and excelled in had been abolished through severe downsizings in the music industry. With the world on hold, I decided it would be a very good thing to attend daily mass.

My attendance at weekly services had been sincere but also discharged the habit and tradition of my Catholic upbringing. Daily mass was something new. I'd never had the time to attend, since travel into New York City required an early departure.

Most of the attendees at those masses were "regulars." Al was; he shuffled in, stopping along the way to greet buddies and share a good morning with parishioners scattered around the church. He sat for a few minutes to greet the Lord, and then rose to light the candles on the altar—certainly not a big job, but Al's attention to the lighting was special. He made sure the candle was straight and the wick not too long. He invariably started on the left side and moved to the right, then went to the center of the altar and bowed.

One morning, Al stopped to say hello to me. Although I attended mass weekly, I usually went to Saturday night five o'clock mass—rushed in and left after the final blessings. I'd never stopped to chat, since I really didn't know anyone. The daily regulars thought I was a new parishioner. Al was the only one to welcome me into that special group. Soon I met his wife Lena. They had been married for forty-nine years and lived most of them in the town of Leonia, in Bergen County. Their three children, by then adults, had attended the local Catholic school.

Soon I was sitting with Al and Lena at daily mass. Without knowing who I was or what they were getting into, they invited me into their home for tea. They listened and we shared stories of our lives. In no time at all, we were fast friends.

It is remarkable how, in such a short time, this friendship moved to a place of special love. Al sat quietly in the living room while Lena and I chatted away. When we shared a cup of tea, he joined us. They listened through my job-search struggles and the realities of my cancer diagnosis. We began to call each other, not out of obligation, but to check in. The entire process seemed right.

This past spring, Al developed difficulty breathing. He had worked all his adult life in an environment that affected his lungs. Soon he developed pneumonia. At eighty-one, he had Parkinson's disease, too. Trips back and forth to the doctor resulted in several hospital stays. Lena, always proud, went to visit daily, but more importantly, was his medical advocate.

Soon he was sent to rehab. The stays in the hospital slowly took little bits of him away. The last several weeks were the most difficult. Although the doctors only said he might have, we believe Al suffered mini-strokes. His ability to speak was affected. Walking and standing became increasingly difficult. Through it all, though, he smiled at Lena and said he was doing OK.

This past week, he stopped eating. The doctors recommended two options: a feeding tube, or hospice. Lena choose hospice at the home. She planned to move Al's bed down to the living room, so friends and family could come visit and that his last days would be filled with love and attention from those who knew him.

Lena and I spoke on a Thursday; she planned to relocate the bed on Friday and bring Al home on Saturday. I had treatment on Friday, so we did not speak again. Usually when I have treatment, I do not sleep that night—the drugs seem to stir me up. Around five to four in the morning, I woke with thoughts of Al and Lena in my head. I reached for my rosary and said a rosary for Al and then one for Lena, promising myself I'd visit the next day. Saturday I have a standing appointment with David, the healer I work with in Montclair. When I got home, there was a message from Lena. Her voice was very quiet; Al had passed during the early morning, around 4:00 a.m. They planned a one-day wake at the local funeral home, and then mass on Wednesday at 10:00 a.m.

Harvey and I went to the wake on Tuesday. The room was filled with flowers and people coming to pay respects to that quiet man of dignity and love. Lena, dressed in black, stood strong. Pictures of their life together had been arranged on tack boards around the room. One in particular, showing Al at his son Danny's wedding, took center stage. His smile just beamed. It was the total essence of him.

I attended Mass on Wednesday; the daily regulars came to share that last event with Al and his family. I sat behind the family section, knowing that, as much as my heart told me they were family, I was a newcomer to their circle. The casket was carried in, and then the family. Lena kept her eyes straight until she saw me, and then she reached out a hand, which I took and squeezed. I cried lots of tears for my dear friend, for the life she had shared and the one she would now have. She had told me the evening before that, with all her planning, she'd never thought it would end this way. I could not go to the cemetery.

I must confess that, through this difficult time for my friends, my thoughts are selfish. I project my own funeral. I cannot help but wonder if faith and belief in an afterlife can help lessen the grief of the loss. Sitting in the packed church, the dominant image was of the coffin with Albert's body inside. The quiet sobs, the specially selected reading, all spoke to a glorious resurrection, a return to the ultimate home, a joining with the Father.

I realize that faith is not supposed to be selective, though my doubtful thoughts are not what I expect. Thoughts of dying and leaving this world—loved ones, my Harvey—have been floating in my head since the initial diagnosis. I have not slept very well. I write this to honor Albert, but also to assist in the process of my own grieving. If I believe that this life is only a temporary stop, that the body is just one phase of the soul's journey, Al is still with us, just in a new form that, although we do not see it, exists concurrently with us. Is this wishful thinking? Is this a loss of faith? Is this the reality of surrender? I don't know. I only know my heart hurts for my dear friend Lena, and for myself, over the loss of a special man.

An Encounter

IT'S BEEN WEEKS SINCE I have attempted to write. Truth be told, I have been busy with living. Each day we go to the gym. We work with weights for about half hour and do a half hour or so of cardio work. This is essential and part of my personal plan for survival. The workout is to keep my body strong. There are days when I just cannot lift the lowest weights, and I start to cry. Harvey is there to remind me that there are some people at the gym who are healthy and are not as committed as I am. I shake off the frustration but remember a time when this was not the case.

I have come to recognize an amazing feature about time. The more you have, the more you are capable of filling in. Sometimes I stand back from the day-to-day and realize that I have adjusted to an entirely new life pattern. It's certainly not the pattern I would have chosen for myself or my life with Harvey, but it is a pattern nonetheless.

I am well aware of my physical limitations. I am committed to make decisions about activities that bring me a sense of joy and accomplishment.

I have started to teach a Leadership class at Montclair State University. I love working with the students. Most are full-time and working. The class is scheduled in the last cycle, so most of the attendees are exhausted by the time they arrive.

This semester I have been honored to have several former students in my class. One returning student is Andres. He attended my Human Resource Management class. Andres is from Colombia, living in the U.S. these past eleven years with his mom. He works forty hours a week at the deli counter of Pathmark. He is a serious student and active in university activities that contribute to the overall community.

This semester he is taking six classes and has requested permission to audit mine. This simply means he will not be responsible for the assignments. I have approved his appeal and requested his active participation in class discussion.

At the end of the first class Andres waited for me. He commented about my hairstyle change. I'd made myself a promise not to lie about my circumstance. As my wig was now short, he asked what had made me cut my hair. I breathed deeply and replied it was not my choice, that I had been undergoing treatment at Sloan Kettering and that this was a result.

It's interesting to watch people's reaction to the mention of Sloan. Andres got very serious and asked if it was breast cancer. We were walking to the parking lot when I told him it was pancreatic. He stopped, took my hand, and asked me if he could pray for me. I was touched by his response and of course told him that would be fine. Before he walked away he hugged me. I felt good about this encounter and remarked about it when I got home.

The next morning on email there was a message from Andres. He told me how very saddened he was with the news of my condition. That he cared deeply for me and wanted to let me know if he could assist me in any way, he was there for me. I began to cry. I have included his e-mail since I can not do justice to his expression of caring:

> *Hi Professor Rappaport:*
>
> *Tonight as I was walking to my car I felt a deep sadness within me that was letting me know how much I care about you, and I thought to myself, God has His own ways to let us know that we should be thankful for every second that we live and every little thing that we have. And I just felt the need to write you this email to tell you that you are a very strong person and with the help of God you will prevail. I am more than honored to have such an inspiring person like you as my professor, and just so you know you can count on me for anything you might need.*
>
> *I will see you next Monday and God bless you.*
>
> *Andres*

Since the start of this journey there have been some remarkable moments—connections to people I would never have expected to understand or reach out to me. I am strengthened by Andres' offer to pray and help. It is the stuff of living a full life.

We

THOUGH IT'S MY NATURE to make friends easily, I've lately become more private, not wanting to expose my vulnerability and limitations. A few select friends have taken the interest or time to understand what Harvey and I have been going through.

Most people have a surface understanding of cancer. They equate one cancer with all. Most of the time when anyone asks how I am doing, I act as if everything is fine. I have days that are not black-and-white, though, but varying shades of gray—somewhere in my consciousness where I am pretending to be OK but the color of life is muted.

This past weekend Kathi and Roger, friends from Atlanta, visited. I've known Roger for over fifteen years. I originally hired him as the marketing vice president of Weight Watchers. During my career at H. J. Heinz, I'd had the opportunity to relocate him several times. As we hauled our way through the complexities of moving residences and accepting new work assignments, Roger and I got to know each other outside work. His first marriage had produced two children. Lynn, his first wife, had never wanted to relocate from their comfortable home in Maryland. Nor had she wanted the children to visit. Roger, deeply saddened by these decisions, eventually divorced her.

His current wife, Kathi, was a former colleague. She'd never married, and when they reconnected it had been a dream come true.

Kathi has become a dear friend. She has a passion for sending cards and finds the most uplifting sentiments to convey on them. If the card is blank, her own words unfailingly offer encouragement and love. She calls me at least once a week, and we share our stories—from simple household repairs to what's happening in her marketing research business, to movies, books, and theater.

They were in New York for one of Roger's business meetings. Each time he has one here, he's arranged for a visit. This time, Kathi joined him to spend the day with Harvey and me.

The afternoon flew by quickly over family stories and comments on world events. We had dinner reservations at the local Thai restaurant. (They've been missing their Thai fix since their favorite one in Atlanta closed.) After dinner we came back to the house for tea and dessert.

The atmosphere was mellow. Although Kathi knows all about the trials and tribulations of my treatment and passes it on to Roger, he had never asked for details directly.

Suddenly he hesitantly did, about my treatment protocol. He explained he didn't want to bring up the subject if we were uncomfortable answering. Harvey gave him enough details for a reasonable understanding. The topic changed, and the balance of the evening again eased. After kisses and expressions of friendship and love,

Harvey drove them back to the city.

Several days later, Kathi called to tell me about their safe flight and their private conversation. Roger'd noted that, throughout Harvey's description of my treatment, he'd used the pronoun *we*. This had struck Roger as something special, and Kathi remarked that not all spouses would have approached the enormity of our life circumstance with the same sensitivity.

Ever since, I have been contemplating what makes my own relationship so very unusual. Yes, it's the two people who come to the marriage—but there is something much deeper. The realities of our current circumstance are all part of our daily lives.

In the beginning the chemo grind took its toll: I was being overly forgetful, distracted, or blue for days. I said, "Sorry, lovey." It had not been not part of our life plan, and I felt I had messed up, not just my life, but ours.

Harvey banned such talk. He's always said, "We can do this."

Harvey's the one who conducted all the research. His hours on the internet provided an invaluable source of detailed information to absorb and ponder. We could manage cancer in print better than in the body. We were armed and ready to ask thoughtful questions about my diagnosis.

We never discussed who would handle what responsibilities or tasks. We instinctively fell into our current pattern of living. We certainly had not planned or anticipated this chapter in our lives but understood we were in it together.

Perhaps it's our soon-to-be twenty-nine years of married life, perhaps the fact that we were friends before we became lovers, or the early impediments resulting from our different ethnic and religious traditions. I only know that we are still deeply in love. When we have our disagreements, we never go to sleep angry or not talking. We have enough sense to know when the other needs private time and space, when not to push beyond the current discussion, to know the subtle signs requiring a different tack for understanding.

We is the word that emerges at a time of great stress between two people whose approach to life is nothing short of teamwork. It manifests itself in sentences like "We have chemo tomorrow" or "Next week we have a scan." We prompt each other for questions we want to ask the oncologist: What side effects have been particularly bothersome, how many nights have gone by without sleep. Cancer is a clever adversary, biding its time—sometimes for years—to break through the body's defenses. Having it is like playing a game of chess with the Angel of Death. One may never reach checkmate, just a protracted stalemate.

Harvey has not missed one treatment or doctor's appointment. And make no mistake—if you are fortunate enough to have someone close with whom to share this nightmare, the first person plural is an entirely appropriate way to describe your good luck.

The Strings of Friendship

I HAVE COME TO see more than ever that we only exist in relationship to others. It is revealing, too, to discover who you are to another person—exposing what we perceive, think, feel, and need. Such honest dialogue can be very difficult, as well as threatening, because it means opening up to another person. Yet this communication develops trust.

I have been surprised, moreover, by how relationships and conversations change when you are not in good health, and I have often thought how effortless friendship seems, especially compared to family. Just showing up qualifies you for a medal.

Consider Eileen. It took us almost two years to talk about anything more important than the weather. The friendship slowly developed to sharing family stories, going to dinner and theater, or stopping by for a cup of tea. Now Eileen is out of my life. I think I know why: Too many of her friends and family members have been diagnosed with cancer, and she's terrified—not just for me but about her being there for me.

There's Grace, who works at the nail salon I used to frequent. At first Grace and I developed a bond around fashion and jewelry. She operated the small booth with specialty items in the salon. When I worked, I was quite a fashion maven. Items from Grace were always different and cutting edge. Over the years, we visited each other's homes. Through each of her pregnancies, I helped out whenever I could. Her reaction to my health news was shattering. Each time she called, she would cry uncontrollably. I finally told her the time for tears was over, that I had made a choice about how I was going to live my life. Once I told her that we were all dying but that my death could be a bit more finite, her calls became less frequent; each began with an apology for not visiting or calling and ended with a promise to make time the following week. It's been two years, and still no visit.

Kathi is the wife of a former colleague at work. She calls weekly and sends cards the sentiments of which feature courage and inspiration. We speak of household chores, movies, theater, books, the pets, and just plain living. She has visited whenever she has an opportunity to fly in from Atlanta. I look forward to her calls—they rarely dwell on illness.

Carolyn, a high school friend, came back into my life about five years ago. Back in the day, we were best friends. Our paths separated after school, she attending college and I going into the business world. She is dealing with her own serious illness, and I'm the only one who knows. She's a single woman who occupies her time visiting friends, caring for her elderly mother, and working about a job she detests. Her calls are always filled with suggestions and ideas on how I can feel better. Sometimes she barely listens to my side of the conversation; her chatter is breathlessly constant. We are lifetime friends, though, and will be there for each other.

Dickey, another former work colleague, has been on medical leave for several years. She has recurring lymphoma, is reliant on pain medicines, and is uninterested in trying alternative healing methods. Recommendations about taking yoga or meditation classes fall on deaf ears. She calls when she is lonely or has received more bad medical news. I am embarrassed to say, when the phone rings and I see her caller ID, I often choose not to answer. But although, at times, she brings me down, she also shares the experience of living through a life-threatening illness. She understands the ups and downs.

Of course there are others who write cards and call periodically, always with the preface that they think of me often but hesitate to call or intrude.

My men friends are amazingly less complicated. They call, inquire about my condition, and move on to what's happening in the world and their lives. Their conversations stimulate my brain. We reminisce about the days we worked together and how good they were. They always ask how Harvey is doing.

I hardly think of myself as a high-maintenance person. Pondering these relationships has led me to understand that friendships are like strings. Some are thin and tend to stretch and break away; others are elastic and withstand the distance of time and silence. Those that break away are meant to.

Most of us pride ourselves on our self-sufficiency. We like to be responsible for pulling our own weight in the world. This is why it can be so challenging when we find ourselves in a situation in which we have to rely on others, which is what happens in the case of an illness. At times like these, we must let go of the feeling that we should be able to do it all by ourselves, and accept the help of others no matter in what form. Upon reflection, all of the people I've mentioned here, and others I haven't, have attempted to reach out a hand in their own way. People come into our life for a reason, a season, or a lifetime. When you know which one it is, you know what to do. When they walk away, I now realize that our need has been met, their work is done, and it is time to move on.

Sleep

Will I Know?

I HAVE ALWAYS BEEN a voracious reader. While I was working, my fantasy was to read all day long. Now that my life has shifted and I find myself with more time, I am interested in even re-reading some books. Something mysterious happens when your eyes see, your ears hear, differently. You attend to what you have been ignoring. The experienced world actually changes shape. With changed eyes, I want to see if my perspective has been altered.

Recently I started to re-read the Old Testament. In all my years of religious education, whenever I read the story of Eden the focus was on the Tree of Knowledge—the forbidden instruction which lost us Paradise. And what was Paradise? The Tree of Life—life immortal. Yet although we don't like to think about it, no one exits this world alive. It's a part of the human condition that is usually ignored. Yet you can't think about living without thinking about dying, even if it's only in the recesses of your mind.

My personal philosophy includes the notion that what you focus on becomes your reality. Has my diagnosis shifted my view more toward life? Since it's more precious, is everything colored with a vibrancy that I didn't notice before?

Helen Keller wrote: "I seldom think about my limitations, and they never make me sad. Perhaps there is just a touch of yearning at times; but it is vague, like a breeze among flowers."

This statement rings true to me. I still mourn for the me I used to be, but it's getting less now. I have accepted this new living. Most of us struggle our entire life to be complete, to be successful, be the greatest we can be, to achieve our potential. Most of us end as we entered this world, kicking and screaming—afraid of the unknown. The rare few who get the bigger picture, who know that life on the planet is about learning and connecting to each other, who see beyond the self to a community of shared experiences and love, exit with grace.

When I can't sleep at night, my mind moves to these thoughts. I believe we are more than just our physical body, that the essence of who we are, our consciousness, our soul, moves to a grander place. Some call it heaven, some the universal force field. I am not sure about the details, but I do not believe we vaporize. Harvey and I have discussed this. He believes life is what it is. That we are meant to be the best we can, and then it's over. I wonder if I will know when it is my time. Will I know when to stop the chemo, the Pollyanna smile when I am in pain? Will I know when? And will I exit with the grace of knowing I have become the best I was meant to be? I can only wonder.

Insomnia

I've read that, as you get older, you need less sleep. I am not sure this is true for me or a result of the chemo; particularly of late, though, sleep has been elusive. It takes forever for me to fall asleep, and then in an hour or two I'm wide awake.

Many nights I've lain in bed beside Harvey, barely touching his back with my arm, waiting for the darkness to pull me in. I've tried all the remedies people suggest—melatonin, red wine, exercise, meditation, chamomile tea. None of them seem to work. They make my body drowsy, but not my mind. My mind is a roulette wheel, rattling and spinning in endless circles, never quite landing on one spot.

Could this restlessness be an excess of consciousness—an excess of life? I can't will myself to shut it down. Dreams, if there are any, I rarely remember, or they're filled with bogey men and monsters.

I shuffle down the stairs, pull a throw blanket from the closet, and attempt to settle on the sofa. I hear the chimes of the grandfather clock on the hour. I stop focusing on not sleeping. I read until dawn.

My eyelids are heavy. The cats have nestled around me. I concentrate on my breathing. Finally I lose myself. I shift my position. The chimes tell me it's 6:00 a.m. How long can a person survive without sleep? Am I dozing during the night and just not aware of it?

    I resolve to speak to Dr. O'Reilly. Of course there is yet another pill to induce sleep. Yet another medicine. Not sleeping can't be a good thing, can it? I begin to cry. I wake to find tears on my face. Thank God it's a new day.

Life and Death

Just a Movie

LAST NIGHT WE SAW the movie *United 93*, a dramatization of the fourth plane to be hijacked on 9/11. The writer/director/producer respectfully depicts the last hours of the doomed crew and passengers. The cell phone calls to family and loved ones only speak of love. The goodbyes are heart-wrenching.

The Eastern mystics say we choose the manner of our death before we are incarnated to this earthy existence. In their sacrifice, the passengers of United Flight 93 chose to be messengers to the world, particularly the United States. In their final hours, status, prestige, annual bonuses, counted for naught.

Thoughts of dying filled my head through the night. In many ways, a life-threatening illness creates an amazing freedom—to be able to stand up and leave everything behind—without looking back. To say *yes*: *Yes* to life is, at one and the same time *yes* to oneself—without pretense. *Yes*—even to that element that is most unwilling to let itself be transformed from the reality of now to the uncertainty of the unknown.

We'll See

I have learned to step back and start saying, "We'll see," instead of judging the events in my life as good or bad, right or wrong. I recognize that, in itself, nothing is good or bad, and that everything has the potential to help us get back on the universe's schedule. This does not mean that we have to like what's happening, simply that we must remain open to the uses even of adversity.

A disease may serve as a redirection—a reset button.

When you learn to live your life with a "we'll see" attitude, you understand how it is that disease can be considered a gift.

I am grateful just to be alive. I am glad to have been permitted to learn to live with, rather than simply die from, cancer. Mostly I am glad to measure my life, not in terms of what it once was or what I might have wished it to be, but of how wonderful it is now. I am glad to recognize each day as splendid.

John Lennon wrote, not long before he was gunned down: "Life is what happens to you while you're making other plans."

Each human being is a unique creature whose passage through the life journey expresses only the view from its own vantage point. We are not born "finished." Inner growth is possible as well as the outer development mediated by nature and experience. Step out of yourself and see your center, your still point—a second perspective, one that is always calm, alert, detached, tuned in, but not overshadowed. Life is neither predictable nor linear.

Mortal illness, like most personal catastrophes, comes on suddenly. You have no great sense of premonition. You just wake up, visit the doctor, and suddenly encounter a new clarity — knowing each day is a gift, that time is limited, and that, when you wake each morning, you know in a profound way you have just one right dance to live this day, your aim to string days together, moments, into a life of achievement and purpose.

Cancer made me want to do more than just live. It made me want in live in a certain way. Time has gotten slower as my awareness of life's details has increased. I no longer have lists of things that must be done. I have a new annoying habit of not making decisions because any decision is usually the correct one in that moment. It's not a matter of not caring but of grasping that anything is just fine with me as long as it is part of living in the now.

If you pay attention to the present, what comes later will also be better. Forget about the future; live each day according to the flow of the universe, confident that God loves his children and that each day, in itself, brings with it an eternity.

Wherever your heart is, there you will find your treasure, for life attracts life.

Who Am I?

FEBRUARY 2, 2007—IT'S twenty months since I was diagnosed. Lately I have been feeling more tired than usual. The cumulative effects of continuous chemo are beginning to take their toll. Yet I am so very blessed. When I initially met with my original oncologist I naively asked, "How long?" He looked at me and smiled a sad smile. He could be accurate to a point; lots depended on my reaction to the drugs, how fast the tumor would grow, my mental attitude...I pressed him further. It was important for me to know what I was dealing with. Finally he acquiesced and stated clinically, this was a virulent, fast-growing cancer, and given that I was at the fourth stage—perhaps a year. So that was the prognosis.

Dr. O'Reilly, who took over early on, has been pleasantly surprised, and, truthfully, so have we. After the shock and the tears, I decided I would not die of a diagnosis—that statistics were averages, and I was bold to declare that Rose Rappaport had never been average a day in her life. Whether it's my gene pool (my paternal grandmother lived to be 104), my insistence that I keep to a fully active life (I teach at the university and continue to consult on an at-call basis), my support system of family and friends requesting calls for prayers and positive thoughts, or my darling Harvey, who refuses to let me stay in the dark cave of my mind too long—I know I am blessed, yet my heart is heavy

My friend Terri called several nights ago. We met her at our vetinarian's office. She was the able assistant who calmed our precious cats during their examinations. Her luminous blue eyes reassured our angst. A single woman in her mid-thirties, Terri stroked and soothed in a manner that was engaging, not only to our cats, but to us two-legged beings. Soon we became friends and engaged her to cat-sit for us whenever we traveled. And she loves cats. We know her visits will include not only feeding and litter box patrol, but squeezing and petting our three furry children.

Terri had called to tell us that the breast cancer that had in remission for two years earlier had invasively returned. Her recent scans showed a growth on her liver and nodules in the bones of her shoulders, neck, and chest. She was calling to ask for a recommendation for a second opinion. We talked for a long time. I listened carefully, allowing her to say what she was feeling. I offer words of courage, knowing what her new battle will entail.

Cancer, cancer, cancer. It never becomes a meaningless noise the way almost any other word does when you repeat it endlessly. There is something about the way the letters hang together that is oddly malignant. The cure, with its well-documented cumulative effects, knocks you down like a ton of bricks or flattened like Road Runner under an Acme safe.

How one handles a life-threatening illness demonstrates character. Cancer has brought me two lives: one as a healthy person, and another as a—what? I don't know what to say, for I have never claimed this diagnosis. What is my identity in the face of so radical a disruption? Who was I? Who am I? Who will I be? Truthful answers to these questions often take years to realize. I am on a fast track—always was—but now the movement forward is different. I cannot run and hide. Sometimes I wish I could be less introspective, less aware of what's going on inside.

Suffering does different things to different people. Some souls become tempered, unshakable in their trust in God; others become twisted and misshapen, abandoning all connections to Him.

Like school, each medical test or procedure is another determinant of your fate. Passing the test or getting a bad grade has few do-overs. When you flunk, you die. Hearts, lungs, bones, blood—the raw materials that keep you alive—are so very vulnerable. They wear out, wear down. But the spirit—that is another story. In many ways my soul has gotten stronger, experiencing life with more wisdom and gratitude. Yes, I am blessed more today than before because the spirit can shine beyond the realities of the body.

I believe this because it sustains me.

Surrender

ONE OF THE MORE amazing elements of this journey has been my total surrender to the Will of God. I realize that, for some readers, this statement sounds like I have given up or am delusional. I am far from a Holy Roller or an evangelical.

The idea of total surrender is a new one for me. I was raised Catholic and attended grade school, high school, and college with religious instruction. I was fortunate that my teachers, nuns or priests, always provided a platform of self-discovery and constant questioning. My attendance at mass or Holy Days is not driven by guilt or habit, but by choice. Jesus Christ is alive for me, and I believe I am where I am supposed to be.

This was not always the case. In September 2001, before 9/11, I was downsized from a position as Vice-President/Human Resources in the music industry. It was a job I loved and was good at. World events after 9/11 exacerbated a slowing economy. My expertise was attached to a high price tag, and efforts to explain I was willing to start over met with the corporate cold shoulder. In the midst of this fruitless job search, I attended a parish mission. Frustrated and close to despair, I met Fr. Daniel Francis, a Redemptorist priest. His words and passion about the Christ rekindled the smoldering embers of my faith. Fr. Dan spoke of the Lord's passion and death as the anchor for resurrection and revival.

I'd always had an eclectic reading regime, but now I wanted to fill myself with reading from both the West and East. Eastern philosophy and Zen Buddhism merged together with readings of Aquinas, John of the Cross, and Theresa of Avila, simmering diverse yet similar messages of trust, faith, and love. These imprints reinforced my personal philosophy, which, simply stated, is "you create the world you live in."

I had a choice, therefore, about how I would deal with my diagnosis and live the balance of my life, no matter how long. The concept of surrender is foreign to Western sensibilities, particularly in the U.S. Yet the intentionality of accepting life's circumstance takes an enormous burden from your being.

For me surrender, aka acceptance, did not mean I would *give up*. I researched my illness and actively participate in my treatment. My oncologist, Dr. Eileen O'Reilly, is one of the special experts who has the sense and style to ask me what I think about what's happening to *me*.

Surrender gives up the struggle of anger and denial. It understands there just may be no other "reason" than circumstance. Surrender allows me to take control of my thoughts and actions. It places trust in a Higher Power—whether my higher sense of self, or the Universe or God. It provides, at least for me, a booster shot on the days the pain is too strong and I am scared.

A terminal illness takes over your life, but acceptance allows me to boldly state: *"I will not die from a diagnosis."* My spirit is buoyed up to plan for the future and to live in hope.

Last Notes

THE LAST WEEKEND HAS been a rush of activities yet as I rest in the hospital bed, we are moving at a snail's pace.

Friday I insisted on chemo although Dr. O'Reilly, in her always settled manner, was recommending not to. She is a terrible poker player. My appointment include a walk-in appointment for ultrasound of my legs, as I have been concerned about blood clots, and an appointment with Dr. Markowitz a gastroenterologist. The disease is spreading.

I spent the weekend in pain, arguing with myself over whether to go to urgent care or not. Without sleep for three days, I am in urgent care. Cannot say I lost.

In many ways, the body knows. Dr. O'Reilly came to see me on Monday. She wanted to speak to me alone regarding arrangments for hospice. There appears to be inflammation in the left lung—could be from the disease, could be inflammation from the radiation, could. . . .

I started this essay in hope several weeks ago and have been unable to complete it. I think this just might be the time.

About the Author

Rose Alfano Rappaport was born into a traditional Italian Catholic New York City household in 1948. As women of her place were not encouraged to higher education, her achievements of attaining associate's, bachelor's, and MBA degrees (each with honors) were truly significant. Each degree was achieved through evening and weekend classes while always holding down a full-time job. Rose began her Human Resource career at CBS. Succeeding positions were at Home Insurance, ADP, AIG, HJ Heinz, and BMG Entertainment. She always had a motivation to give back. Early in her career she was an adjunct professor at Saint Peters and Dominican Colleges. After she left BMG, she began her consultancy, Human Capital Partnership, and returned to college teaching at Montclair State University. A voracious reader, she wondered about her own voice. Shortly after she started taking writing classes, she was diagnosed with pancreatic cancer. Writing about her experience became the compelling mission that eventually resulted in *Living In Parentheses*.

www.ingramcontent.com/pod-product-compliance
Lightning Source LLC
Chambersburg PA
CBHW022133080426
42734CB00006B/343